I would firstly like to dedicate this book to ALL of my wonderful Instagram followers! Without your constant encouragement and support I wouldn't be here today, fulfilling my dream of publishing my very own cookbook filled with wholesome, colourful recipes.

I would also like to specially dedicate this book to my partner, Alex. You have been the biggest help – assisting me in setting up shoots, cleaning up the many messes and, most importantly, helping me eat all of the food in this book … even the failed recipe attempts.

ELSA'S
Wholesome
LIFE

ELLIE BULLEN

plum.

Pan Macmillan Australia

CONTENTS

INTRODUCTION

Hi! My name is Ellie and I'm a nutritionist and dietitian. Some of you may know me from my recipe blog and website, Elsa's Wholesome Life, where I share all of my favourite recipes and other tips that celebrate healthy food and healthy living.

I've always loved eating fresh, nutritious food and living a fun, adventurous life. I grew up in Lennox Head, a small Australian beachside town close to beautiful forests and lush farmland. I guess you could call me a foodie. I love going to the local farmers' market and buying my ingredients from local growers. I also love supporting small businesses, such as my local bulk wholefoods shop and family-run grocer. Shopping at these places makes me feel good and allows me to source new and interesting ingredients to incorporate into my recipes. I also love to travel, trying different cuisines in different cultures and then experimenting with those flavours and ingredients in my own cooking.

I believe we live in a world where food has become way too convenient, and many of us have lost the art of cooking and experimenting in the kitchen. Most of the ready-to-eat 'food' on our supermarket shelves is far from nutritious, high in bad fats and sugars and low in nutrients, yet it is heavily marketed and widely available. I think this is one reason why so many people find it hard to make healthy food choices. I have written this book in the hope that it will inspire more people to get back into the kitchen and learn how to cook real, healthy, wholesome foods.

Personally, I adore plant-based foods – veggies, fruits, whole grains, nuts, seeds and legumes. Their gorgeous colours and amazing textures make them so much fun to prepare, plus eating them just makes me feel so damn good! I literally bounce out of bed with the sun and have heaps of energy throughout the day.

As you will see from my recipes, I choose to exclude meat, eggs and dairy from my diet. In part 1 of the introduction, I talk about why eating this way feels

so right for me. Part 2 explains how to make the most of a plant-based diet, ensuring it includes enough protein and minerals such as iron and calcium. Part 3 has some of my best tips for becoming super confident in the kitchen, including meal prepping, shopping well and having the right utensils. And in part 4, I talk about other really important aspects of a wholesome life, including keeping fit, relaxing and sleeping well. Then it's on to my delicious recipes. I'm thrilled to be able to share these with you – they're super healthy yet also happen to be very easy to make. Plus they taste awesome! I've also included lots of basics such as dips, sauces, non-dairy milks, bread and pasta, which are simple to make and will really ramp up your confidence in the kitchen.

I hope that by reading this book you'll feel empowered to make healthier food choices, knowing that you can easily prepare your own foods instead of relying on over-processed food. And, of course, my other secret wish is that you'll be inspired to include more plant foods in your diet.

WHY A PLANT-BASED DIET?

I haven't always followed a plant-based diet. Five years ago there weren't many foods I didn't eat, and although I'd always try to eat healthy foods, I was uneducated and ill-informed and tended to get drawn into trying fad diets and nutritional supplements. The first things to go were meat and dairy, though I continued to eat seafood. A year later I gave up seafood, too, as it didn't feel right. I continued to eat eggs occasionally, but only when I could be 100 per cent sure that they were from an ethical source. This meant I didn't eat any packaged food or restaurant meals that contained eggs, as I could never be sure that they had been produced humanely.

Some of you may wonder if I miss the foods I have excluded, and the answer is a resounding 'No!' I love plant-based foods and here's why:

A PLANT-BASED DIET IS GOOD FOR YOUR HEALTH

Quite simply, vegetables, legumes, whole grains, fruits, nuts and seeds contain everything your body needs for optimum health and vitality. Together, these foods have plenty of carbohydrates for energy, as well as heaps of vitamins and minerals, including crucial nutrients such as vitamin C, folate, zinc and magnesium.

Plant-based diets are also high in fibre, which means you'll have no issues going to the loo! Fibre is not only great for intestinal health (regular bowel movements reduce your risk of digestive issues and bowel disease), but it also ensures you have plenty of 'good' bacteria in your gut – and a healthy gut microbiome is linked to a great array of health benefits, most notably immune function.

A plant-based diet is naturally lower in fat, particularly the kind of saturated animal fat that is not good for your health. But you still get plenty of healthy fats from olive oil, nuts and seeds. As for protein, combining legumes, such as chickpeas and lentils, with grains, such as rice and oats, ensures a complete source of protein. I also use a lot of nuts in my cooking, as they contain good amounts of protein, fibre and minerals. Population studies have shown that people who eat a handful of nuts every day appear to have a reduced risk of heart disease – though this effect may be due to the fact that they are eating fewer sugary snacks because they're eating nuts instead.

Actually, I'm quite happy not to eat red meat, as research suggests that it may play a role in the development of colorectal cancers. In fact, the World Cancer Research Fund International's recommendations for cancer prevention include eating more plants and less meat.

A PLANT-BASED DIET IS GOOD FOR THE ENVIRONMENT

The livestock industry is actually the largest contributor to environmental damage today. This includes pollution, water use, land use, species extinction, antibiotic resistance and fish species depletion. Animal husbandry, in fact, produces more greenhouse gas emissions than the transport sector, which is mostly due to the methane gas production from livestock (methane is 25–100 times more destructive to the ozone layer than carbon dioxide).

Reducing your meat and dairy consumption also means you use less water, more so in fact than you would save from taking shorter showers and recycling grey water. This is because raising animals for meat and dairy products requires enormous amounts of land to grow their feed, which in turn requires irrigation. According to the makers of the documentary *Cowspiracy*, it takes 9500 litres of water to produce 450 grams of beef – about four burger patties. Pretty shocking! Why don't we just use that land and water to grow our food instead?

Another environmental aspect to be aware of is 'food miles', which refers to the distance your food travels from its source to your plate. I always try to buy local and seasonal produce, that way I know it hasn't taken a ship, plane, train, truck and car to reach my tummy and therefore has less of an impact on the environment. Try shopping at your local farmers' market or greengrocer – though always ask where they source their produce.

A PLANT-BASED DIET IS HUMANE TO ANIMALS

I will openly and honestly say that ethical considerations did not initially drive my decision to follow a plant-based diet, but protection of the environment and the humane treatment of animals are now the biggest factors that sustain my passion. Factory farming is the number one cause of animal cruelty worldwide and, unfortunately, the demand for meat has meant the development of factory farming on a massive scale. Indeed, about 70 per cent of the worldwide production of poultry is from factory farming, along with 50 per cent of the pork, 40 per cent of the beef and 60 per cent of the eggs. This means that many animals are raised in dire conditions, such as overcrowded cages or pens with no access to exercise or fresh air, plus they may be fed poor-quality feed that contains growth hormones, antibiotics or other chemicals.

However, we are not powerless to change this situation; we get to vote with our dollar. If we buy less meat and choose ethically sourced foods, producers will have to respond to demand. Of course, I'm not saying everyone should eat only plants. That's just not realistic, nor is it fair. But even if families were willing to have one day each week where they ate no meat, it would be of enormous benefit not only to their own health but also the health of the whole planet. If you are interested in learning more, these documentaries are incredibly informative: *FoodInc, Forks over Knives, Cowspiracy* and *Earthlings*.

MAXIMISING YOUR NUTRIENTS

While a plant-based diet is uber healthy, you need to ensure you are getting enough iron, calcium and vitamin B12, as well as the right balance of macronutrients (carbs, proteins and fats).

GETTING ENOUGH IRON

Our bodies need iron to make red blood cells, which transport oxygen to our body tissue and organs. Iron is important for maintaining our energy levels and keeping our mood stable.

There are two types of iron in food: haem iron and non-haem iron. Haem iron comes from animal products (mainly red meat), and non-haem iron comes from plants. Adequate iron intake is particularly important for women, who lose iron in their monthly cycle. We actually need twice the amount of iron (18 mg per day) than men do, and our requirements are even higher during pregnancy (27 mg per day). In fact, iron deficiency is the most common nutrient deficiency in the world, especially among young women. And it is not always related to diet.

Unfortunately, non-haem iron is less bio-available (which means it's not as easily absorbed by the body), so we plant-based bunnies need to be really aware of our iron levels.

Iron-rich plant-based foods include:

- Legumes (beans, peas, lentils)
- Nuts and seeds
- Soy products (milk, tofu, tempeh)
- Grains
- Dark leafy green vegetables (spinach, silverbeet, broccoli, bok choy and kale).

Fortunately, there are things you can do to improve the bio-availability of non-haem iron:

1 Eat iron-rich foods with vitamin C–rich foods such as tomatoes, sweet potatoes, citrus fruits and berries (vitamin C assists iron absorption).

2 Always soak your grains, legumes, nuts and seeds overnight to break down the phytates. Phytic acid is found in the hulls of all nuts, seeds and grains and is basically a form of phosphorus, which helps plants grow. However, in our bodies, phytic acid tends to bind to minerals like iron, zinc and calcium, making them less bio-available. (See Soaking Grains, Legumes, Nuts and Seeds on page 18.)

3 Consume small amounts of iron-rich foods across the whole day, as your body doesn't absorb large, single doses well.

If you don't think you are getting enough iron from dietary sources, have regular blood tests with your GP (every three to six months) and if your levels are too low, consider an iron supplement or infusion.

GETTING ENOUGH CALCIUM

Calcium is a crucial mineral for maintaining strong bones. It is also important for efficient muscular contractions (including your heart!), nerve signalling and blood clotting. A healthy amount of calcium in your blood is vital, and your body will forfeit calcium from your bone stores if you are not getting enough. This means that a simple blood test will not tell you if you have enough calcium stored in your bones, which can put you at risk for osteoporosis later in life. For this reason, I would recommend you have a DXA (bone density) scan, to make sure you have healthy levels of bone minerals.

The main dietary source of calcium is dairy foods and small boney fish, such as sardines. Some plant-based milks are fortified with calcium, and you may like to fortify your own homemade nut milks with calcium supplements. I do this rather than take a supplement, as nutrients are best absorbed when consumed with other nutrients at mealtimes across the day.

Plant-based foods high in calcium include:

- Leafy green vegetables
- Nuts and seeds
- Fortified cereals, non-dairy milks and tofu.

SOAKING GRAINS, LEGUMES, NUTS AND SEEDS

In all of my recipes, particularly when I'm making cashew cream, raw cakes, nut milks and fruit and nut loaves, I like to pre-soak my grains, legumes, nuts and seeds. This means placing them in a bowl or a jar, filling it with at least double the amount of water and leaving them on the bench or in the fridge to soak for at least eight hours. (You can cover them with a cloth or lid if you prefer.) I like to soak mine overnight, so I usually leave them for twelve hours or more. When ready to use, I drain them in a strainer and rinse them under fresh water. Even if I'm going to cook rice, buckwheat, oats, dried beans or peas, I always follow this process. When I cook grains, I often add additional water as they tend to soak up the water very quickly.

But why should you soak grains, nuts, seeds and legumes? Well, soaking not only softens them, making them faster to cook and easier to blend into creamy pastes, but also decreases the phytate content (the anti-nutrients that block our ability to absorb minerals), which means they are more nutritious.

After the soaking process, you can even try sprouting your beans, grains, nuts and seeds. Simply leave them in a strainer over a bowl at room temperature, rinsing them daily until they're sprouted.

Another soaking-related tip involves using seeds such as flax and chia to make a vegan egg replacement. I generally go by the rule of 1 teaspoon of seeds to 3 teaspoons of water, and always soak for 10–15 minutes to allow the seed and water to form a gelatinous mixture (just like an egg!).

GETTING ENOUGH VITAMIN B12

This vitamin plays an important role in red blood cell formation, brain and nervous system function and DNA replication, but can only be found in animal foods (meat, eggs, dairy). This means vegans must include some food sources that have been fortified with vitamin B12. My favourite is nutritional yeast, which I add to dips and sauces or sprinkle on my dinners. Some store-bought cereals and veggie patties are also fortified with B12 – check the ingredients label.

This is another nutrient that you'll need to keep track of with your GP or dietitian, and consider taking as a supplement if your levels are too low.

BALANCING YOUR CARBS, PROTEINS AND FATS

Vitamins and minerals are micronutrients because we only need them in tiny amounts. Macronutrients, on the other hands, are the nutrients that we need in large amounts i.e. carbohydrates, proteins and fats.

Carbohydrates

Many people think the term 'carbs' refers to foods like bread and pasta, and that we shouldn't eat them. But carbohydrates are actually found in almost every food except meat and eggs. They're in grains, fruits, vegetables, nuts, seeds and even dairy products, and are the preferred fuel source for our brains and bodies. We just need to learn to eat the right kinds of carbs and in the right amounts.

Carbohydrates, or saccharides, are sometimes grouped into 'simple' and 'complex'. Simple carbs, commonly known as sugars, include the monosaccharides glucose, galactose and fructose and the disaccharides lactose and sucrose. Because they are small molecules, they are digested and absorbed quickly into the bloodstream, which can cause rapid spikes in blood sugar. Foods high in sugar are typically packaged foods like soft drinks, chocolates, confectionary, biscuits, cakes and pies, as well as sauces, condiments and sweeteners. These have what is known as a high glycemic index (GI) and, depending on how much of them you eat, they can also have a high glycemic load (GL).

Complex carbs are made up of hundreds or thousands of simple carbs joined together in tight structures. There are two main types of complex carbs: starches and fibre. Starches are found in vegetables, such as potato, sweet potato and sweet corn, and in grains, such as oats, wheat, rice and rye. While it takes longer for the body to break down starches, they are also eventually converted to glucose.

Fibre, on the other hand, is the name given to the parts of plants that are resistant to digestion in the small intestine (we do not have the enzymes to break them down and absorb them into our bloodstream), so they hang around the colon, where they bulk up our stools and help to feed friendly bacteria.

There are two types of fibre: insoluble and soluble. Insoluble fibre helps build up your number twos, while soluble fibre attracts water into the colon and helps soften your stools, so they exit more easily. Basically, fibre is great for keeping your bowels regular and healthy. Fibre in food also slows digestion, helping to delay spikes in your blood glucose, as well as trapping fats from being absorbed. Processed grains have had the outer layer of bran removed (e.g. white flour, white rice), meaning they have less fibre and more starch and are quickly converted to glucose in the body. This is why I prefer to eat whole grains, such as oats and brown rice.

Okay, now let's talk about sugar. No matter how you dress it up, too much sugar of any kind is not good for your body. It doesn't matter if it's fructose-free, unrefined or highly refined – it's still sugar. And unless you need that sugar for a bout of intense exercise, it's going to get stored as fat or hang around the body and mess with your insulin levels.

After a great deal of research and study, I have decided that it's okay to use a little bit of sugar in my cooking, but it needs to be in the most natural form possible: dates, bananas, berries or sometimes a little maple syrup.

Yes, I am pro-fruit! And if anyone tries to tell me 'you shouldn't eat lots of fruit, it's full of sugar', I'm quick to react. Yes, fruit does contain fructose, but it is also packed with nutrients (especially vitamin C and other antioxidants), fibre and water. Plus it is sooo delicious! So I say, eat your fruit, and even though dietary guidelines recommend we have just two pieces of fruit per day, if you are a four-pieces-a-day kinda gal don't panic – it's so much better for you than snacking on packaged chocolate bars and cakes.

I love to use dates in my recipes because they have such a creamy caramel sweetness, yet have all of their nutrients and fibre intact. You can buy them fresh, semi-dried or dried. My absolute favourites are medjool dates. These are usually found in the fresh food section of the supermarket or in bulk wholefood stores. However, I still treat these guys like sugar: one medjool date contains around 3 teaspoons of sugar, so keep this in mind when you're adding them to smoothies.

The other way I like to sweeten my recipes is by using overripe fruit, such as bananas, mangoes and papayas. As fruits ripen, the resistant starches turn into simple sugars and they become sweeter and more easily digested. You can usually pick up discounted bags of overripe bananas from greengrocers or fruit shops.

Protein

Protein is important, not only for building muscle but also for growing our hair and nails, making enzymes and hormones, and even making our red blood cells.

Our bodies break down all the protein we eat into amino acids (I like to think of them as little building blocks), which are then used to grow and repair tissues and to create the enzymes and hormones we need for digestion and myriad other functions. There are 21 different amino acids, nine of which are essential, meaning our bodies cannot synthesise them from other amino acids and we must get them from our diet.

Now, I'm sure anyone who is vegetarian or vegan has been asked where they get their protein from. The answer is legumes (peas, beans and peanuts), nuts, grains and seeds, all of which contain plant protein. All we need to do is to eat a good variety and quantity of these foods. Individually, most of these plant foods do not contain adequate levels of all nine essential amino acids, so they are known as incomplete proteins. Legumes, for example, are very low in methionine, but grains have plenty. Conversely, while grains are low in lysine, legumes have good levels. For this reason, I pair my legumes, such as lentils, with a grain, such as rice. That way I know I'm getting all nine essential amino acids. This is known as a 'complete protein' source.

Most people need about 1 gram of protein per kilogram of body weight. The best plant-based sources of protein are soy products, since soy beans (aka edamame) are a complete source of protein. Products made from soy beans include tempeh, tofu and soy milk. I love tofu and tempeh, as they are really versatile and can be added to most dishes. Chickpeas are my second favourite source of plant-based protein (I am hummus OBSESSED!). Chickpeas can also be used in curries and veggie patties or dried and ground into flour for baking. Quinoa is

another complete plant protein, containing all nine essential amino acids, so makes a great addition to a vegan or vegetarian diet.

In most of my recipes, you will see that I combine different legumes and grains, and that I try to add at least one protein source to each meal. Adding ingredients such as hummus, cashew cheese or peanut butter is a sneaky and delicious way to boost the protein. These foods also make really healthy snacks between meals. In addition, you can buy plant-based protein powders that can easily be added to recipes. I usually purchase plain pea and rice protein powders from my bulk wholefood store and mix them together to make a complete protein source.

Fats

Eating healthy fats as part of every meal is really important. Our bodies need fat. In fact, every single cell inside your body has a surface layer of fats (a lipid membrane), and since we are constantly replacing our cells an intake of fats is essential. Fats help to keep your skin and hair beautiful and healthy, too. They also help you to absorb the fat-soluble vitamins A, D, E and K from your foods.

Scientists always seem to be arguing about which types of fats are bad for you and which are good for you, though the general consensus has always been that saturated fats (found in meat, dairy and some plant oils, such as coconut and palm oil) are considered 'bad', and unsaturated fats (from plants, nuts and seeds) are considered

'good'. This is because saturated fats are more readily stored as fat in the body and less easily used as fuel, leading to raised levels of bad cholesterol (LDL), which in turn can lead to fatty deposits in your blood vessels and an increased risk of cardiovascular disease.

While this sits nicely with a vegan diet, it's not as simple as saying 'all unsaturated fats are good'. Firstly, there are two types of unsaturated fats: monounsaturated and polyunsaturated. Monounsaturated fats are abundant in olive oil, avocado, almonds, cashews, macadamias and eggs. These fats raise the levels of good cholesterol (HDL) in your blood, decreasing your risk of heart disease, which means they should be enjoyed as part of a balanced diet.

Polyunsaturated fats are found in seeds and seed oils (sunflower, safflower, flaxseed, sesame), legume oils (soybean and peanut), fish and walnuts. Two types of polyunsaturated fats, omega-3 and omega-6, are known as essential fatty acids, because we have to get them from our diet (our bodies can't synthesise them from other fats). And when it comes to getting adequate amounts of these fatty acids, balance is key. The desired ratio of omega-3 to omega-6 is somewhere between 1:5 to 1:10. As these two fatty acids compete for absorption, having an excess of one can impede the absorption of the other.

It's very easy to get adequate omega-6 (linoleic acid or LA) from our diet, as it's found in sunflower oil, safflower oil, grapeseed oil, soybean oil, rice bran oil and anything labelled 'vegetable oil'. In fact, it is estimated that we are consuming up to 25 times more omega-6 than omega-3.

There are several different types of omega-3 polyunsaturated fatty acids. Alpha-linolenic acid (ALA) is a short-chain omega-3 fatty acid commonly found in plant foods, notably flaxseeds (linseeds), chia seeds, pumpkin seeds, walnuts, canola and legumes. However, our bodies need to convert ALA into docosahexaenoic acid (DHA) and eicosapentaenoic acid (EPA), which are the long-chain omega-3 fatty acids important for cardiovascular protection and immune function. This means we need to consume good amounts of plant-based omega-3s (ALA) and reduce our intake of omega-6s (LA).

When cooking, I always use good-quality cold-pressed olive oil and sesame oil – they are my absolute must-haves. Nutritionally, olive oil is my favourite, as it is mostly monounsaturated fat and contains very little LA and saturated fat. Sesame oil has a really beautiful flavour, and I love adding it to Asian dishes. But even if I didn't cook at all, I'd still get plenty of healthy fats from all the avocados, seeds and nuts I use, especially in nut milks and nut and seed spreads (e.g. tahini, peanut butter etc.).

Coconut oil is often considered great for cooking, as it has such a high smoke point. Although it is high in saturated fats, these are mainly from lauric acid, a type of saturated fat that is believed to act differently from other saturated fats by increasing good cholesterol (HDL).

However, some studies have shown that it may also increase bad cholesterol, so until there's more solid evidence, I'm on the fence with this one. I do, however, use coconut oil in some of my treat recipes as these are 'sometimes' foods, and even though they are super nourishing and nutrient dense, I'm not advocating you guzzle loads of them. Plus, coconut oil gives raw treats an amazing flavour and texture.

TRANS FATS

Trans fatty acids (TFA) are created when unsaturated oils are partially hydrogenised to make them solid at room temperature. Food manufacturers then use them to increase the shelf life of processed foods like pies, pastries, cakes and biscuits. TFA not only increase LDL (the bad) cholesterol, but also lower HDL (the good) cholesterol.

Trans fats are also created (albeit at much lower quantities) when vegetable oils are re-used for deep-frying. The structure of the unsaturated fat becomes unstable and, to put it simply, acts like a saturated fat in the body. Trans fats are commonly found in processed food, margarine and deep-fried takeaway food. This is another reason I love to make my own food.

GETTING ORGANISED
IN THE KITCHEN

While it's great to understand how to balance nutrients for optimum health and wellbeing, the real key to a healthy plant-based diet is being organised in the kitchen. Knowing the healthiest foods to eat won't guarantee you will eat them, especially if you come home from work or uni to an empty fridge. The only way to resist the temptation of processed and fast foods is to have a well-stocked pantry and fridge and to plan a few of your meals ahead.

SMART SHOPPING

I do my grocery shopping once a week and always have a list with me, so that I get the right ingredients for the recipes I want to cook. I love to walk down to my local farmers' market on Saturday mornings to pick up seasonal fruits and vegetables, and I always get a coffee and fresh juice on the trip. I buy all of my wholefood staples from a plastic-free bulk wholefood store. I just bring in all of my labelled jars and fill them up with nuts, seeds, flours, whole grains, dried herbs and ground spices. I also drop into various locally owned fruit and veg shops throughout the week to pick up any extra ingredients I need. Buying from small local businesses is really important. Not only does this reduce your carbon footprint, but it also supports people in your local community.

MEAL PREPARATION

Preparing meals in advance is super important for healthy eating. If you have ingredients ready to go and snacks prepped for the week, then you won't find yourself reaching for unhealthy convenience foods. I like to prepare some ingredients or dishes over the weekend. I'll usually bake a batch of granola, a loaf of banana bread or a batch of muffins so breakfast is sorted. I also like to make a healthy snack to take to work, which might be homemade muesli bars, a fruit and nut loaf or my apple pie muffins. In the winter months, making up big batches of soup (such as my pumpkin or green soup) is really handy for speedy lunches and dinners. Another thing I always do is soak the nuts needed for a batch of nut milk for the week and some chickpeas to make hummus.

Although I like to think of a few different meals to have in the coming week (so I can buy the right ingredients at the markets), I also love to come up with creative dishes by using what I have in the fridge and pantry. Leftovers are usually my lunch the next day, or I'll throw together a really big salad.

I also tend to go through little food obsessions, especially when my weeks are really busy. For example, I remember a time when I was having chunky baked pumpkin, hummus and steamed green veggies every night for a couple of weeks. This makes life very easy, though it may not work so well if you have others to cook for!

I also buy bananas and mangoes when they're overripe and on sale at the fruit shop. I buy a heap, peel them and freeze them, ready for smoothies.

PANTRY STAPLES

There are a few ingredients that are absolute essentials in my pantry, and I always make sure I have them at the ready:

- oats (for a cheap breakfast, for baking and for smoothies)
- brown rice (add to basically any lunch or dinner)
- split lentils (cheap and quick to cook)
- almonds (great for snacking and making almond milk)
- peanut butter (homemade or store-bought; add to your smoothies, drizzle over sliced fruit or make yummy dipping sauces and salad dressings)
- cashews (keep these handy for making vegan cheese sauces)
- olive oil (for baking, grilling and dressing salads)
- tamari (I add this to many dishes for a tasty salty flavour)

- apple cider vinegar (stir into your morning water or use for salad dressings)
- sesame seeds (sprinkle over stir-fries, salads, cooked veggies, dips and dipping sauces)
- spices (ground cinnamon, cumin, paprika, chilli flakes, black peppercorns)
- nutritional yeast (check to see if fortified with vitamin B12).

I wish I could say that I grow all of my own veggies in a big organic garden in the country, but that's just a dream for me at the moment. Though I do grow rosemary, basil and sage in pots on my balcony. Growing herbs is relatively easy and a great idea, as often you only need a handful for a dish. I also grow edible flowers, such as pansies, marigolds, violas and nasturtiums, to use in my food styling. They look so pretty on dishes, brighten up my balcony and are so easy to grow.

COOL UTENSILS

There's no doubt that having the right tools for the job makes life much easier in the kitchen. These are the utensils I couldn't live without.

Blender

If you're as passionate about plant-based foods as I am, you'll want to get yourself a high-powered blender. I looove my Vitamix, and I use it many times a day. It allows me to make really thick and creamy nice-cream, nut butters, nut milk, raw cakes, smoothies, flours and soups. Do your research and buy the most powerful one you can afford. I can honestly say it will be worth the investment.

Spiraliser

The next thing I use all the time is my spiraliser. I love using it to make veggie pasta ('zucchetti'). A spiraliser makes super-long, curly veggie strips and most have two blades, one for making flat, wide ribbons and the other for thin 'noodles'.

Julienne peeler

This is really useful for shredding carrots, cucumbers and zucchini for salads, wraps and rice paper rolls. You can also use it to make veggie pasta if you can't get your hands on a spiraliser.

Cold-press juicer

Cold-press juicers gently crush fruits and vegetables to release their juices, while the high-speed action of other juicers creates heat that damages some of the nutrients. I've had my juicer for five years now, and it's *so* handy! It even allows me to get juice from leafy green veggies, such as spinach and kale. Plus, I get to keep the pulp for baking cakes and muffins, making veggie patties or just for composting (it's a great fertiliser).

Non-stick frying pan

A good-quality non-stick frying pan is invaluable. Not only does it ensure you don't overuse oil in your cooking, it also makes flipping pancakes or frying veggie patties much more enjoyable. I only use wooden and silicone utensils to prevent scratching, and I replace the pan once the non-stick layer begins to peel. I've been using marble pans recently, too – they work really well with only a tiny bit of oil. I have also read great things about stoneware and cast iron cookware, so if you can afford these options consider investing in them.

ENJOYING A HEALTHY LIFESTYLE

As life seems to get busier and more complicated, we rely more on short cuts and convenience: instead of walking or riding a bike, we drive cars or take public transport; we do our shopping online and have it delivered to our door; or we drive through fast-food outlets or order home delivery, so that we don't have to think about shopping and cooking. And while some of these things do make life much easier, taking care of our health is something that shouldn't be outsourced. So far, I've talked about the importance of eating the right balance of nutrient-dense foods, but you also need rest and exercise to make the most of your healthy diet.

EXERCISE

I like to move my body until I sweat for at least an hour every single day. I think keeping fit is really important for long-term health. I do loads of cardio, such as running and high-intensity interval training, in order to maintain a strong and healthy heart. I also love doing yoga and pilates weekly to stretch and strengthen my body.

For me, working out is not a chore. I do my run, yoga or pilates first thing in the morning, so that I feel full of energy and have the happy endorphins flowing all day. Once you find something you enjoy doing, just make it part of your routine. And it doesn't need to involve expensive classes or equipment – it can be as simple as walking to the greengrocer instead of driving or riding your bike to catch up with friends. You will absolutely fall in love with how good you feel afterwards.

Alex, my partner, and I also have a bit of a ritual where we go for an hour's walk at sunset to catch up on each other's day. While studying and writing this book, I was fortunate to be living on a fairly central part of the Gold Coast, so on weekends I was able to walk to the markets, my fave cafes and restaurants and to the beach. But wherever you live, you will have options for walks, rides and other ways to keep moving.

RELAXATION

A healthy body isn't just about eating well and working out. It's also about having a healthy mind. We need to make time to relax and enjoy ourselves.

Everyone has different ways they like to relax. For me it's yoga and meditation. After a yoga class, I always have this internal feeling of calmness that stays with me for the rest of the day. I also have a mindfulness app that I listen to when I'm commuting to uni on the train. Even sitting on my couch on the balcony surrounded by all my plants and listening to music relaxes me.

Slotting in just 5–10 minutes a day to meditate has really amazing effects on your brain. Other things you might like to do are: walks in nature (they call this green therapy!), run a bath, light some candles, read a book or lay on the beach and listen to the waves.

SLEEP

When people talk about a healthy lifestyle, they often forget how important it is to catch those zees. A good sleep routine will improve your energy levels, stabilise your mood and make it easier to concentrate. Plus, it allows your body to do all its repair work, which amps your immune function. I know how this works from personal experience. I used to stay up late studying (for some reason my brain seems to function well at night), but I'd still want to get up early (I'm a 5 am kinda person). I was going through long periods of not getting enough sleep, so whenever I got a break my body would crash and I would end up sick. I've now realised that I need to get at least 7–8 hours of sleep each night, and so I make an effort to get myself to bed earlier. This means that after dinner I try to put my laptop away and relax on the couch. (Working on a screen late at night messes with our circadian rhythms, and it's much harder to switch off and go to sleep.) You may find reading a book in bed or listening to some gentle music is a good way to wind down, or, if you're a hard case, try setting an alarm to remind you that it's bedtime!

A WONDERFUL DAY STARTS WITH A NOURISHING BREAKFAST

PEANUT-NANA BREAD

This is basically banana bread with a nutty twist. The peanut butter makes this loaf moister, higher in protein and, most importantly, more delicious! I love mine warmed up and topped with freshly sliced banana.

1 tablespoon flaxseeds
1 cup (150 g) wholemeal spelt flour
1 cup (150 g) unbleached self-raising flour
2 teaspoons baking powder
1 teaspoon bicarbonate of soda
⅓ teaspoon salt
1 tablespoon ground cinnamon
2 bananas (230 g peeled), plus 1 small extra for topping
¼ cup natural peanut butter (see Tip page 286)
110 g medjool dates (about 6), pitted
1 cup soy milk or other non-dairy milk (see recipes page 279)
¼ cup extra-virgin olive oil

Preheat the oven to 170°C fan-forced (190°C conventional) and line the base and sides of a 20 cm x 10 cm loaf tin with baking paper.

Place the flaxseeds and 3 tablespoons of water in a bowl. Stir well and set aside.

In a separate bowl, sift together the flours, baking powder, bicarbonate of soda, salt and cinnamon.

Place the two bananas, the peanut butter, dates, milk and oil in a blender and blend until smooth. Add the mixture to the soaked flaxseeds and stir well to combine.

Make a well in the centre of the dry ingredients. Add the wet ingredients and stir until just combined. Pour the mixture into the prepared tin. Slice the extra banana in half lengthways and place on top. Bake in the oven for 45–60 minutes, or until a skewer inserted in the centre of the bread comes out clean.

Remove the bread from the oven and leave to cool in the tin for 20 minutes before transferring to a wire rack. Allow to cool for a further 20 minutes, then slice into eight thick pieces. Serve toasted with a smear of coconut oil, sliced banana, and a drizzle of maple syrup.

Store in an airtight container in the fridge for up to 10 days.

SERVES 8

HERBY PUMPKIN BREAD

This bread is my absolute favourite. It is *so* moreish! I think it's the pumpkin and herbs that have me hooked. Pumpkin is rich in beta-carotene, the precursor for vitamin A, which is important for eye health. Since vitamin A is a fat-soluble vitamin, it's more easily absorbed when combined with fats, so I like to serve this bread with avocado or hummus (see page 300 for a recipe).

1 cup (150 g) wholemeal spelt flour
1 cup (150 g) unbleached self-raising flour
2 teaspoons baking powder
1 teaspoon bicarbonate of soda
½ teaspoon salt
2 cups grated pumpkin (about 250 g)
1 tablespoon dried rosemary
1 tablespoon dried thyme
⅓ cup extra-virgin olive oil
1 tablespoon flaxseeds
2 tablespoons pumpkin seeds

Preheat the oven to 180°C fan-forced (200°C conventional) and line the base and sides of a 20 cm x 10 cm loaf tin with baking paper.

Sift the flours, baking powder, bicarbonate of soda and salt into a mixing bowl. Stir in the grated pumpkin and dried herbs.

In another bowl, combine the oil, flaxseeds and 1 cup of water and stir well.

Pour the wet ingredients into the dry ingredients and stir until just combined. Transfer the mixture to the prepared tin and sprinkle with the pumpkin seeds. Bake for 50–60 minutes, or until a skewer inserted in the centre comes out clean.

Remove the bread from the oven and leave to cool in the tin for 15 minutes before transferring to a wire rack. Allow to cool for a further 30 minutes, then slice and serve fresh or toasted with homemade hummus or sliced avocado sprinkled with chilli flakes.

Store in an airtight container in the fridge for up to 10 days.

SERVES 8

TIP
*This savoury bread is perfect
for dipping in soups.*

THE FRUITIEST NUT LOAF

Every time I bake this I tell myself I have to do it more often! It's *so* full of goodness and loaded with flavour and crunch. This isn't like a store-bought fruit loaf where you have to go hunting for the raisins – it's chock-full. The nuts, seeds and dried fruit will keep you going all morning. I've used buckwheat flour so that it's gluten free, but feel free to substitute with plain wholemeal or spelt flour if you're okay with gluten.

1 cup (150 g) buckwheat flour
1 teaspoon baking powder
1 teaspoon bicarbonate of soda
1 teaspoon ground cinnamon
pinch of salt
2 cups dried fruit (figs, apricots, raisins, cranberries),
    roughly chopped
1 cup nuts (pecans, walnuts, almonds), pre-soaked
    (see page 18) and roughly chopped
½ cup seeds (pumpkin, sunflower), pre-soaked (see page 18),
    plus extra for topping
¼ cup extra-virgin olive oil

Preheat the oven to 180°C fan-forced (200°C conventional) and line the base and sides of a 20 cm x 10 cm loaf tin with baking paper.

Sift the flour, baking powder, bicarbonate of soda, cinnamon and salt into a mixing bowl. Add the dried fruit, nuts and seeds and toss to combine. Pour in the oil and 1⅓ cups of water and stir until the ingredients are just combined. Transfer the mixture to the prepared tin and sprinkle with the extra seeds.

Bake for 50–60 minutes, or until golden on top and a skewer inserted in the centre of the loaf comes out clean.

Remove the loaf from the oven and leave to cool in the tin for 15 minutes before turning out onto a wire rack. Allow to cool for another 30 minutes, then slice and serve fresh or toasted with a smear of coconut oil, macadamia nut butter or on its own.

Store in an airtight container in the fridge for up to 10 days.

SERVES 8. GF

APPLE PIE MUFFINS

Having a muffin for breakfast is A-okay when they're as healthy as these! This recipe contains no refined sugar but has the perfect amount of sweetness from the sultanas and apples. I have tried to replicate an apple pie with the yoghurt and granola on top – similar to an apple crumble with ice cream. Pie apples are available in the canned fruit section of the supermarket – though always read the ingredients list to ensure they're not loaded with extra sugars. Alternatively, you may like to use freshly grated apple.

1½ cups (240 g) wholemeal self-raising flour
1 teaspoon baking powder
½ teaspoon bicarbonate of soda
1 tablespoon ground cinnamon, plus extra to serve
2 teaspoons vanilla powder
¼ cup rolled oats
⅓ cup sultanas
¼ cup extra-virgin olive oil
1 cup soy milk or other non-dairy milk (see recipes page 279)
1 teaspoon chia seeds
1 x 800 g can pie apples (or 5 apples, peeled, cored and grated)
TO SERVE
coconut yoghurt
1 green apple, cored and finely sliced
granola or toasted rolled oats

Preheat the oven to 180°C fan-forced (200°C conventional) and line a 12-hole muffin tray with paper cases or baking paper (if using a non-silicone tray).

Sift the flour, baking powder, bicarbonate of soda and spices into a mixing bowl. Sprinkle in the oats and sultanas and toss to combine.

In a separate bowl, stir together the oil, milk, chia seeds and apple. Allow to sit for 5 minutes.

Pour the wet mixture into the dry mixture and stir until just combined. Spoon evenly into the muffin tray holes and bake for 30–35 minutes, or until a skewer inserted in the centre of a muffin comes out clean.

Remove the muffins from the oven and leave to cool in the tin for 20 minutes. Transfer to a wire rack to cool for a further 20 minutes. Serve topped with a tablespoon of coconut yoghurt, a couple of fresh apple slices, a tablespoon of granola or toasted oats and a dusting of cinnamon.

Uneaten muffins can be stored in an airtight container in the fridge for up to 1 week.

MAKES 12

SPICED MAPLE-ROASTED
GRANOLA

I solemnly swear that this is the most delicious granola … ever. There is nothing better than the smell of this wafting from the kitchen on a Saturday morning. It's so yummy that sometimes I just pick at all the clusters while I'm waiting for it to cool! Try making up a batch, popping it in a jar, adding a personalised tag and gifting it to someone special.

1¾ cups (200 g) whole pecans, pre-soaked (see page 18)
2 cups buckwheat
⅓ cup mixed flaxseeds and sesame seeds
pinch of salt
2 teaspoons ground cinnamon
½ teaspoon ground cardamom
1 tablespoon sesame oil
1 tablespoon extra-virgin olive oil
¼ cup maple syrup
zest of 1 orange (about 2 tablespoons)
    (reserve the segments to serve)

Preheat the oven to 160°C fan-forced (180°C conventional) and line a baking tray with baking paper.

Place the pecans, buckwheat, seeds, salt and spices in a large bowl and give them a good stir. Add the oils, maple syrup and orange zest and toss until well coated. Spread the mixture evenly over the prepared tray. Bake for 15–20 minutes, or until golden. The granola will firm upon cooling.

Set the granola aside and allow to cool for 5–10 minutes. Serve with the orange segments and some coconut yoghurt, or use as a topper for a smoothie bowl.

Store in a sealed jar in the pantry for up to 2 weeks. (Or keep in the fridge for extra freshness.)

SERVES 12, GF

CHOC-NUTTY 'NOLA

This recipe is for all those choccy lovers who want a fix at breakfast time. My choc-nutty 'nola is very low in sugar (one-third of a date per serving!) and high in protein, fibre and healthy fats. I love this granola with fresh berries and homemade nut milk, or as a crunchy smoothie topper.

2 cups nuts (almonds, cashews, pecans), pre-soaked
  (see page 18)
1 cup buckwheat
2 cups puffed rice
2 tablespoons flaxseeds
75 g medjool dates (about 4), pitted
2 tablespoons natural peanut butter (see Tip page 286)
  or almond butter
¼ cup macadamia oil or extra-virgin olive oil
2 tablespoons cacao powder
pinch of salt
1 cup coconut flakes

Preheat the oven to 160°C fan-forced (180°C conventional) and line a baking tray with baking paper.

Place the nuts, buckwheat, puffed rice and flaxseeds in a mixing bowl and set aside.

Place the dates, peanut or almond butter, oil, cacao powder and salt in a blender and blend until smooth. Transfer to the mixing bowl and stir well until all of the dry ingredients are well coated. Spread the granola mixture evenly over the prepared tray and bake for 15–20 minutes, or until browned and sticky. The granola will firm upon cooling.

Remove the granola from the oven and allow to cool for 30 minutes. Sprinkle over the coconut flakes. Transfer to a sealed jar and store in the fridge for up to 2 weeks.

SERVES 12, GF

GOODNESS BOWLS

1 SUMMER 'NOLA BOWL

I don't know about you, but I'm definitely one of those people who goes through phases of having the same thing for breakfast every single day, especially when I'm really busy. This is my go-to when I need a super-quick, nourishing breakfast before heading out. I love it with berries, kiwifruit, passionfruit or whatever fruit is in season.

½ cup Spiced Maple-roasted Granola (see recipe page 48)
½ cup coconut yoghurt
½ cup fresh fruit, sliced
edible flowers, to serve (optional)

Place the granola in a bowl and top with the yoghurt, fruit and edible flowers (if using).

SERVES 1. GF

2 STRAWBERRY DREAM SMOOTHIE BOWL

In summer, I just can't get enough of smoothie bowls. Sometimes I'll even have them for dinner! The trick is to get the smoothie nice and thick (somewhere between a yoghurt and a sorbet), so that all the fruit and granola sits on top. The other trick is to eat it quickly before it melts in the heat.

2 peeled frozen bananas
5 frozen strawberries
½ cup Cashew Milk or other non-dairy milk
   (see recipes page 279)
2 ice cubes
1 teaspoon pea and rice protein powder (optional)
TOPPING
¼ cup Spiced Maple-roasted Granola (see recipe page 48)
½ cup fresh berries or any seasonal fruit
1 teaspoon coconut flakes
2 teaspoons Berry Nice Jam (see recipe page 292)
edible flowers, to serve (optional)

Place the frozen fruit, milk, ice cubes and protein powder (if using) in a blender and blitz until smooth. Transfer to a bowl and top with the granola, fresh berries or fruit, coconut flakes, jam and edible flowers (if using). Serve immediately.

SERVES 1. GF

3 GREEN TEA BOWL

This has to be one of my favourite smoothies – it's chock-full of nutrients and tastes so good! Matcha powder is made from ground green tea leaves. It's way higher in antioxidants than ordinary green tea because you're consuming the whole leaf rather than just steeping it in water. Plus, there's a cup of spinach in this smoothie, which means you are getting one serve of your five daily serves of veg.

2 peeled frozen bananas
½ cup Almond Milk or other non-dairy milk
   (see recipes page 279)
1 medjool date, pitted
40 g baby spinach leaves
1 teaspoon matcha powder
2 ice cubes
¼ cup Choc-nutty 'Nola (see recipe page 53)
½ cup seasonal fruit, such as fresh berries or
   sliced figs
edible flowers, to serve (optional)

Place the bananas, milk, date, spinach, matcha powder and ice in a blender and blend until smooth. Transfer to a bowl and top with the granola, fresh fruit and edible flowers (if using). Dive right in!

SERVES 1. GF

Eat the rainbow

AÇAI MAGIC

Açai is a South American berry that is high in antioxidants and low in sugar. I love making açai bowls at home as the ones served in restaurants are often too sweet. The sachets I use contain pureed and frozen açai berries, and I get them from my local health-food store. Always buy the pure, unsweetened sachets as they're much more delicious. Sharing an açai bowl with Alex after a day at the beach is absolute bliss! It takes me back to our trip to Hawaii when we had açai every day.

2 x 100 g sachets frozen, unsweetened açai berries
2 peeled frozen bananas
½ cup Almond Milk (see recipe page 279)
2 teaspoons cacao powder (optional)
¾ cup Spiced Maple-roasted Granola (see recipe page 48)
1 mango, diced (or cut into stars using a cookie cutter)
2 tablespoons shredded coconut
2 teaspoons cacao nibs
½ cup fresh berries, sliced

Remove the açai sachets from the freezer and allow to thaw for 5 minutes. Break up the contents by hitting with the back of a knife and empty into a blender. Add the bananas, almond milk and cacao powder (if using) and blend on high until smooth and thick (sorbet consistency).

Sprinkle some of the granola over the bases of two glass jars or clear bowls. Arrange the mango around the insides of the jars or bowls, then scoop in the açai mixture. Top with the remaining granola, the shredded coconut, cacao nibs and fruit. Serve immediately.

SERVES 2, GF

BEAUTIFUL BIRCHER

ON-THE-GO

So, you know how I said that I go through breakfast obsessions? Well, this bircher was one I had for a few months. I would actually be excited knowing I had this breakfast waiting in my gym bag, ready to devour on the train on my way to uni! Eating breakfast is important, as it kickstarts your metabolism, helps you to concentrate, gets your bowels moving and prevents those midmorning sugar cravings. I love how you can prep this brekkie the night before and then grab it from the fridge on your way out the door.

½ cup rolled oats
¼ cup Coconut Rice Milk or Almond Milk (see recipes page 279)
1 tablespoon chopped dried fruit (cranberries, figs, sultanas)
8 nuts (any type), pre-soaked (see page 18)
1 teaspoon chia seeds
1 teaspoon sunflower seeds
1 teaspoon shredded coconut
1 cup sliced or diced seasonal fruit (mango, papaya, berries, kiwifruit, passionfruit, pineapple)

Place the oats in a container (or bowl if you're eating at home). Stir in the milk and ¼ cup of water. Top with the dried fruit, nuts, chia seeds, sunflower seeds, coconut and fresh fruit. Seal the container (or cover the bowl) and place in the fridge overnight.

The next morning, grab a spoon and your breakfast is ready to go!

SERVES 1

CREAMY CHAI-POACHED PEAR PORRIDGE

Porridge is traditionally made from oats and it's a breakfast superfood. It has a low glycaemic index (GI), which means energy is released slowly throughout the morning and your blood sugars won't spike. Wholegrain oats also contain beta-glucan, a type of soluble fibre that can help reduce blood cholesterol levels. I love my oats with these spiced, poached pears on top – so warming and delicious.

1 pear, halved and unpeeled
1 tablespoon maple syrup
1 tablespoon Chai Tea Spice Mix (see recipe page 264)
1 cup rolled oats
1 cup Almond Milk (see recipe page 279)
1 teaspoon vanilla powder
1 teaspoon ground cinnamon
1 tablespoon seeds (chia, flax, sunflower), to serve
edible flowers, to serve (optional)

Place 3 cups of water in a saucepan over a high heat. Add the pear, maple syrup and chai tea spice mix and bring to the boil. Reduce the heat and simmer, uncovered, for 15 minutes.

Remove the pear from the pan and set aside. Strain the cooking water into a jug, discarding the tea leaves and whole spices (keep a cinnamon stick for a pretty garnish if you like). Pour the water back into the pan. Add the oats and bring to the boil over a medium heat. Cook, uncovered, for 5 minutes. Stir in the almond milk, vanilla powder and cinnamon and cook for a further 2 minutes, or until the porridge is thick and soft.

Serve the porridge hot, topped with a pear half (or sliced pear if you prefer), a sprinkle of your favourite seeds and some edible flowers, if desired.

SERVES 2

MATCHA CHIA PUDDING

This chia pudding is another really simple recipe that can be made the night before. Chia seeds are an important part of a vegetarian or vegan diet, as they are a good source of calcium. They also contain ALA, a short-chain omega-3 fatty acid that our bodies can convert into EPA and DHA (the omega-3s important for heart health and brain function). Chia seeds are also really high in fibre, which is why they expand and act like a sponge that soaks up heaps of liquid and forms a pudding-like consistency.

⅓ cup chia seeds
1 cup Almond Milk (see recipe page 279)
1 teaspoon matcha powder, plus extra to serve
½ cup coconut flakes
½ cup halved strawberries
¼ cup raspberries

TIPS

- If making this for one person, you can store half of the pudding in a container in the fridge and have it the next day for breakfast.
- If you prefer, you can replace the matcha with the same quantity of vanilla or cacao powder — it's just as delicious!

Place the chia seeds, almond milk, matcha powder and ⅓ cup of water in a bowl and stir vigorously. Place in the fridge for 10–15 minutes to set.

Divide the pudding between two bowls and top with half each of the coconut flakes, strawberries and raspberries. Finish with a sprinkle of matcha and serve immediately.

SERVES 2, GF

WHOLESOME PANCAKE STACK

We all need to treat ourselves to some pancakes every now and then, right? I love to make these for Alex, firstly because I find flipping pancakes really satisfying and secondly because I enjoy watching him attempt to eat a stack bigger than his belly!

1 banana
1 cup (150 g) wholemeal spelt flour
1 teaspoon baking powder
1 teaspoon bicarbonate of soda
1 cup non-dairy milk (see recipes page 279)
1 tablespoon chia seeds
1 teaspoon vanilla powder
extra-virgin olive oil, for frying

TO SERVE
fresh fruit (berries, sliced fig)
maple syrup
coconut yoghurt (optional)
edible flowers (optional)

Preheat the oven to 120°C fan-forced (140°C conventional). Warm a baking tray.

Place all of the ingredients except the oil in a blender and blitz until smooth.

Lightly grease a frying pan with olive oil and place over a medium heat. Add ¼ cup of pancake mixture to the pan. Cook for 2 minutes, or until bubbles form on the top. Flip the pancake and cook on the other side for 20–30 seconds. Remove from the pan and place on the warmed tray in the oven. Repeat with the remaining mixture, greasing the pan as needed, until you have used all of the batter.

Serve the warm pancakes with fresh fruit and a drizzle of maple syrup, plus a dollop of coconut yoghurt and some edible flowers, if desired.

SERVES 3–4 (MAKES ABOUT 12)

FRUITY FRENCH TOAST

Who would have thought you could use banana instead of egg in this breakfast favourite? The tricks to getting this delicious version just right are to drain off the excess mixture, cook the bread on a lower heat and wait patiently until it's golden and crispy before flipping.

2 bananas
½ cup soy milk or other non-dairy milk (see recipes page 279)
1 tablespoon chia seeds
½ teaspoon ground cinnamon, plus extra to serve
½ teaspoon vanilla powder
oil, for frying
4–6 slices of sourdough bread

TO SERVE
fresh berries (strawberries, blueberries, raspberries)
coconut yoghurt
Gooey Caramel Paste (see recipe page 288)
maple syrup

Preheat the oven to 140°C fan-forced (160°C conventional). Warm a baking tray.

Place the bananas, milk, chia seeds, cinnamon and vanilla in a blender and process until just smooth. Pour the mixture into a shallow bowl and set aside to rest for 10 minutes.

Grease a frying pan with a little oil and place over a medium–low heat.

Dip a slice of bread in the banana mixture, coating both sides. Hold the bread over the bowl to drain off any excess mixture, then place the bread in the pan.

Cook the bread for 2 minutes on one side, or until golden and crispy. Flip and cook for another 1–2 minutes. Transfer to the warmed baking tray in the oven. Repeat with the remaining slices of bread and banana mixture.

Arrange 2–3 slices of toast on each serving plate with a handful of berries, a dollop of coconut yoghurt, a teaspoon of caramel paste, a sprinkle of cinnamon and a drizzle of maple syrup.

SERVES 2–3

HEARTY BAKED BEANIES

Homemade baked beans are such a great way to start your day. Beans are high in soluble fibre, which means they draw water into your number twos, softening them and making you more regular. In fact, population studies show that people who eat beans have a much lower risk of bowel cancer. And once you try this homemade version you'll never go near the sugar- and salt-loaded canned versions again. Here, I've served it with a delicious herb-toasted sourdough.

2 teaspoons extra-virgin olive oil, plus extra to serve
1 teaspoon paprika
1 teaspoon wholegrain mustard
1 small onion, diced
2 garlic cloves, diced
3 tomatoes (about 450 g), roughly chopped
1 tablespoon apple cider vinegar
1 x 400 g can cannellini or white beans, drained and rinsed
salt and freshly ground black pepper
2–3 slices of sourdough bread

TO SERVE
dried herbs (thyme, basil or parsley)
baby spinach leaves
finely sliced spring onion
chilli flakes or finely sliced fresh chilli (optional)

Heat the olive oil in a saucepan over a medium–high heat. Add the paprika, mustard, onion and garlic and stir well. Fry for 3 minutes, stirring often, until the onion is soft and translucent. Add the tomato, vinegar and 2 tablespoons of water. Reduce the heat to medium and simmer, uncovered, for 10–15 minutes, stirring occasionally. Remove the pan from the heat. Transfer the mixture to a blender and pulse briefly (it should be like a chunky sauce).

Return the sauce to the pan over a medium heat. Stir in the beans, season to taste with salt and pepper, cover and turn off the stove.

Meanwhile, brush the bread with the extra oil and toast under the grill until golden and crunchy. Sprinkle with the dried herbs.

Serve the beans over the toast with the fresh baby spinach leaves, spring onion and a pinch of chilli (if using).

SERVES 2–3

SMASHED MINTY
PEA TOAST

Mint and peas are such a yummy combo! Gone are the days when my mum had to force me to eat my peas before I left the table. I now snack on them straight from the freezer. Did you know green peas are also part of the legume family? Paired with a good smear of hummus and some sourdough, you can be sure you're getting a nice big hit of plant protein for breakfast.

½ cup frozen peas
¼ cup roughly chopped mint leaves
1 teaspoon extra-virgin olive oil
2 garlic cloves, diced
2 large portobello mushrooms, sliced
4 slices of sourdough or rye bread
⅓ cup Traditional Hummus (see recipe page 300)
salt and freshly ground black pepper
chilli flakes (optional)
edible flowers, to serve (optional)

Place the peas in a small bowl. Half-fill a larger bowl with hot water and sit the smaller bowl inside it for a few minutes until the peas have thawed a little. Remove the small bowl. Mash the peas with a fork, stir in the mint and set aside.

Heat the oil in a frying pan over a medium heat. Add the garlic and mushrooms and fry for 3 minutes, or until the mushrooms are golden.

Meanwhile, toast the bread slices and spread each with a tablespoon of hummus. Top each with the fried mushrooms and pea mixture. Season to taste with salt and pepper and finish with a sprinkle of chilli flakes and an edible flower, if desired.

SERVES 2

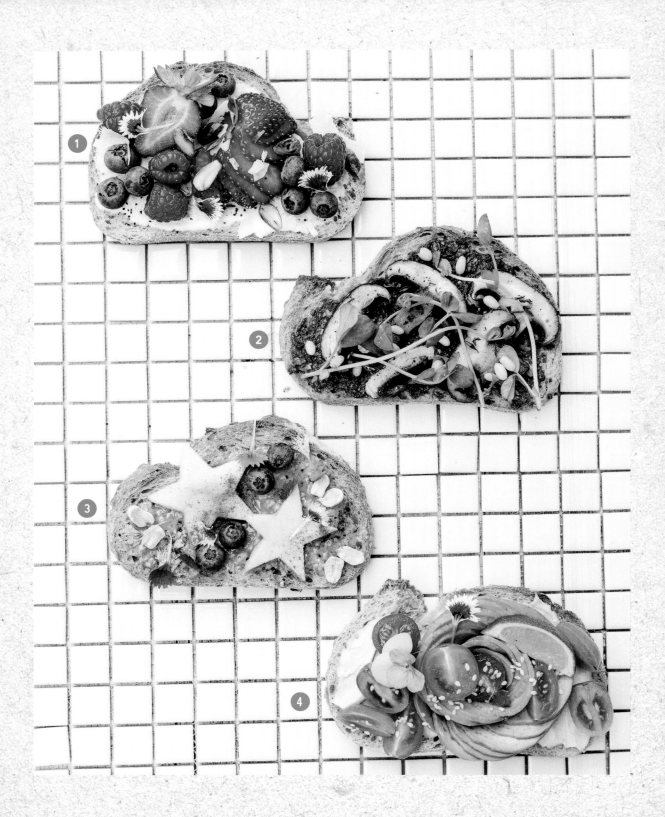

TOAST TOPPERS

This is a fun way to have breakfast. Here are four different topping suggestions, but you can experiment with so many more. I buy my sourdough bread from my local organic bakery, as it's made traditionally (fermented for over 36 hours). The fermentation process makes it easier to digest, as the sourdough bacteria pre-digests the flour, reducing the phytates and making minerals and other nutrients more bio-available. Genuine sourdough should have a sour taste and a chewy texture.

4 slices of sourdough or rye bread

1 BERRY COCONUT
1 tablespoon coconut yoghurt
¼ cup fresh berries (any kind)
1 tablespoon pistachios, chopped
¼ teaspoon poppy seeds
edible flowers, to serve (optional)

2 PESTO AND MUSHROOM
1 tablespoon Super Green Pesto (see recipe page 303)
1 mushroom, sliced and pan-fried in a little olive oil
1 teaspoon pine nuts
snow pea sprouts
chilli flakes

3 APPLE, BLUEBERRY AND PEANUT
1 tablespoon Peanut Sesame Butter (see recipe page 286)
4 blueberries
2 slices of apple
1 teaspoon peanuts, chopped
pinch of ground cinnamon
edible flowers, to serve (optional)

4 AVO AND TOMATO
1 tablespoon Cashew Cream Cheese (see recipe page 285)
½ avocado, finely sliced
4 cherry tomatoes, halved or quartered
1 lime wedge
¼ teaspoon sesame seeds
edible flowers, to serve (optional)

Place all the ingredients on the table in small bowls or in their containers.

Toast the bread slices. Now have fun assembling each creation as listed. Halve each slice of toast so you can try them all!

SERVES 2

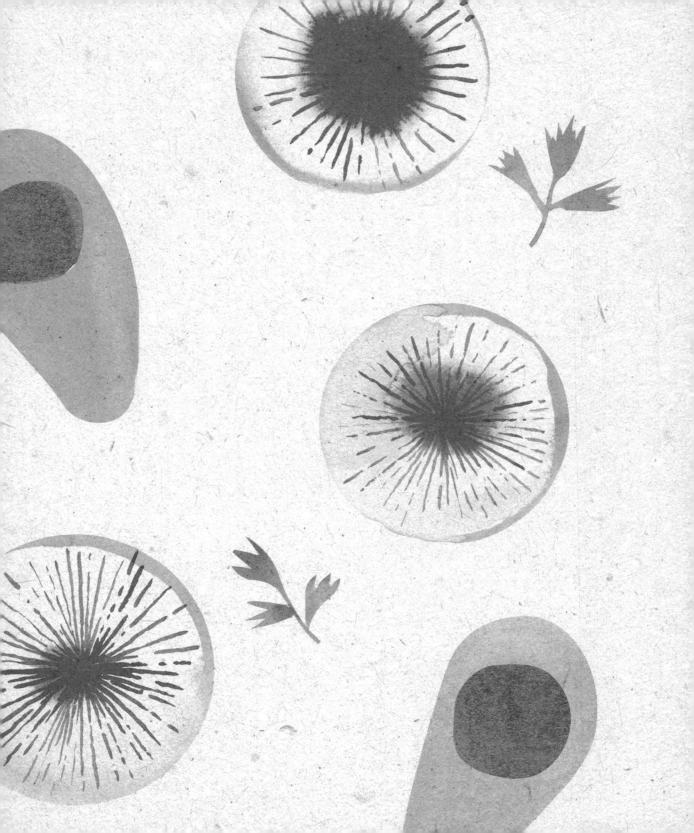

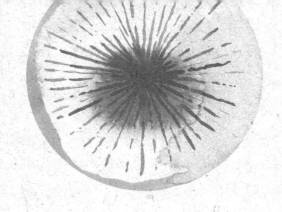

LIGHT MEALS CAN STILL PACK A MEAN NUTRITIONAL PUNCH

SHIITAKE-PUMPKIN DUMPLINGS

I love homemade dumplings, and this combo is a particular favourite. Shiitake mushrooms have a delicious umami flavour, which is why they are often used in vegetarian cooking to give dishes more depth. Plus, recent research suggests that eating these mushrooms improves gut immunity, which can help us fight inflammation. You can make a big batch and freeze up extra dumplings so you have a quick snack or meal ready to go.

350 g pumpkin, peeled, deseeded and roughly chopped
200 g shiitake mushrooms, finely diced
1 bunch of bok choy (about 400 g), finely sliced
1 small bunch of coriander (about 25 g), leaves and stems chopped, plus extra to serve
1 spring onion, sliced, plus extra to serve
1 long red chilli, diced, plus extra slices to serve
2 tablespoons grated ginger
¼ cup tamari
1 tablespoon sesame oil, plus extra for optional frying
30 dumpling (gyoza) wrappers
1 tablespoon sesame seeds, plus extra to serve

DIPPING SAUCE
¼ cup tamari
juice of 1 lime
1 tablespoon sesame oil

Place the pumpkin in a saucepan and cover with water. Bring to the boil over a high heat and cook, uncovered, for 8 minutes, or until the pumpkin is soft. Drain, mash with a fork and set aside.

Meanwhile, place the mushroom, bok choy, coriander, spring onion, chilli, ginger and tamari in a mixing bowl and toss to combine.

Heat the sesame oil in a frying pan over a medium–high heat. Add the mushroom mixture and sauté, stirring frequently, for 3 minutes. Return the mixture to the mixing bowl. Add the mashed pumpkin and stir until well combined. Allow 5–10 minutes to cool.

Place a dumpling wrapper on a clean work surface. Place 2 teaspoons of pumpkin mixture in the centre of the wrapper. Fold over one side to make a semi-circle shape, sealing the edge by pressing with a fork. (Or bring the two sides together vertically, pinching little folds to seal the edges.) Set aside on a large plate. Repeat with the remaining wrappers and mixture.

To steam the dumplings, place them in a single layer in a bamboo steamer over a saucepan of boiling water, cover and cook for 5 minutes. Cook in batches to prevent the dumplings from sticking together.

To boil the dumplings, pour water into a large frying pan to a depth of 1 cm. Cover and bring to the boil. Carefully place the dumplings in the water, ensuring they don't touch, and boil, uncovered, for 5 minutes. (You may need to do this in batches.)

If you like, you can then fry the cooked dumplings. Heat 1 tablespoon of sesame oil in a large frying pan over a medium–high heat. Add the dumplings and fry on one side for 2–3 minutes, or until golden.

To make the dipping sauce, place the ingredients in a jar, seal and shake until well combined. Transfer to a shallow dipping bowl.

Sprinkle the dumplings with the sesame seeds and serve on a platter with extra coriander, spring onion, sesame seeds and chilli and the sauce on the side.

MAKES 30

TIP
*Dumpling wrappers
(sometimes labelled
'gow gee') are made of
wheat and are available
in Asian supermarkets.*

CURRIED SPRING ROLLS

These tasty little delights are nothing like the greasy deep-fried versions you find at takeaway shops — they're baked, not fried. But don't fear, they're still extremely crunchy! Dunk them in some sweet chilli or tamari for instant party food, or serve them as a side with Satay Pineapple Fried Rice (see recipe page 162). Sometimes I'll serve them on top of a crunchy Asian slaw.

1 tablespoon sesame oil
1 teaspoon Chinese five spice
2 teaspoons curry powder
1 onion, finely diced
1 cup frozen peas
1 carrot, grated
¼ small cabbage (about 150 g), cored and shredded
¼ cup tamari, plus extra to serve
12–14 spring roll wrappers
kimchi, to serve (optional)
sweet chilli sauce, to serve (optional)

Preheat the oven to 180°C fan-forced (200°C conventional).

Heat the sesame oil in a frying pan over a medium heat. Add the five spice, curry powder and onion and fry for 2 minutes, stirring often, until the onion has softened and the spices are fragrant. Add the remaining vegetables and tamari and stir-fry for another 2 minutes. Remove from the heat and set aside to cool for 20 minutes.

Place a spring roll wrapper on a clean work surface on the diagonal (one corner pointing towards you). Spoon 2 tablespoons of the mixture in a horizontal line 2–3 cm below the centre, leaving the left and right corners free. Fold the lower edge up and over the mixture and roll to the centre. Fold in each side, then roll up. Place on a baking tray with the loose edge facing down. Repeat with the remaining filling and wrappers.

Bake the spring rolls for 20 minutes, or until crispy and golden all over. Serve hot as they are with a side of kimchi (if using), some little dishes of tamari and/or sweet chilli sauce for dipping, or on top of a crunchy Asian slaw.

MAKES 12–14

TIP

Spring roll wrappers are available from Asian supermarkets and are made from wheat flour, water and salt.

MUSHROOM MEDLEY
SAN CHOY BAU

This is a really simple vegan take on san choy bau – a Vietnamese dish that is typically made with minced meat. Mushrooms are a really great substitute for meat, because they have an umami flavour and an almost 'meaty' texture. I've also added some brown lentils to boost the protein and iron content – key nutrients for anyone on a vegan or vegetarian diet. Even Alex, who claims to hate mushrooms, loves this dish!

1 teaspoon sesame oil
1 tablespoon grated ginger
¼ teaspoon Chinese five spice
300 g mixed Asian mushrooms, diced (see Tip)
1 x 400 g can brown lentils, drained and rinsed
2 garlic cloves, diced
¼ cup tamari
12 lettuce leaves (cos or iceberg)
2 cups bean sprouts (about 150 g)
1 small bunch of coriander (about 25 g), leaves picked
¼ cup unsalted roasted peanuts, roughly chopped
1 lemon, cut into wedges
fresh chilli, sliced (optional)

TIP

Asian mushrooms include shiitake, enoki, oyster mushrooms, straw mushrooms and wood-ear fungus. Look for them at Asian grocers or your local farmers' market.

Heat the oil in a large wok or frying pan over medium–high heat. Add the ginger and five spice and stir-fry for 1 minute, or until fragrant. Add the mushrooms, lentils and garlic and stir-fry for another 2 minutes. Add the tamari and stir continuously for 1 minute. Remove the pan from the heat.

Place the lettuce leaves, sprouts, coriander, peanuts, lemon wedges and chilli (if using) on a platter in the centre of the table. Place the wok alongside. To serve, everyone fills their own lettuce leaf 'cup' with a few tablespoons of the mushroom mix and tops it with sprouts, coriander, peanuts, a squeeze of lemon juice and a pinch of chilli, if desired. Just like tacos, but way healthier!

SERVES 3–4. GF

PESTO-POTATO CROQUETTES
WITH KALE AND RELISH

These little pesto-filled balls of joy make my tummy very happy. This is my gluten-free, vegan version, and it's so tasty! You can even serve these on a platter at a party.

2 large potatoes, cubed
1 zucchini, grated
1 tablespoon nutritional yeast
pinch of salt
⅓ cup Super Green Pesto (see recipe page 303)
½ teaspoon extra-virgin olive oil
100 g kale, stems removed and leaves chopped (about 2 cups)
No-sugar Tomato Relish (see recipe page 330), to serve
small handful of basil leaves, to serve
handful of halved and quartered cherry tomatoes, to serve

Preheat the oven to 160°C fan-forced (180°C conventional) and line a baking tray with baking paper.

Place the potato in a saucepan and cover with water. Bring to the boil over a high heat and cook for 10 minutes, or until the potato is soft. Remove the pan from the heat, drain and mash the potatoes with a fork. Add the zucchini, yeast and salt and stir until well combined.

Take a heaped tablespoon of the mixture and mould it into a ball. Press your thumb (or the top of the tablespoon) into the ball to create a deep cup shape. Place a heaped teaspoon of pesto in the 'cup', then fold over the edges, sealing the pesto in the centre of the ball. Place on the prepared tray.

Repeat with the remaining mixture and pesto until you have about 10–12 balls. Bake for 25–30 minutes, or until golden and crispy on the outside.

Meanwhile, heat the oil in a frying pan over a medium heat. Add the kale and sauté for 3 minutes, stirring occasionally, until wilted.

Divide the croquettes between serving plates and serve hot with a side of kale, a generous dollop of relish and a scattering of basil leaves and cherry tomatoes.

SERVES 2. GF

THAI PUMPKIN SOUP WITH
SALT AND PEPPER TOFU

This is the soup for those wintry nights when you just want something to warm you up like a big hug. Pumpkins are *super* high in beta-carotene (a plant-based precursor of vitamin A) and contain less starch than sweet potatoes (which is useful to know if you are trying to reduce carbs). It actually tastes better the next day, as the spices become more flavoursome, so take any leftovers for lunch — just take the tofu in a separate container and add it to the soup right before you eat it.

1 tablespoon sesame oil
1 onion, diced
2 garlic cloves, diced
1 teaspoon ground cinnamon
1 teaspoon ground nutmeg
1 teaspoon ground turmeric
2 kg butternut pumpkin, peeled, deseeded and chopped
½ teaspoon salt
freshly ground black pepper, to taste
1 x 400 ml can full-fat coconut milk
coriander leaves, to serve
1 spring onion, finely sliced, to serve

SALT AND PEPPER TOFU
2 teaspoons sesame oil
250 g firm tofu, cubed
2 teaspoons sesame seeds
½–1 long red chilli, sliced
¼ teaspoon salt
½ teaspoon freshly ground black pepper

To make the soup, heat the oil in a large saucepan over a high heat. Add the onion, garlic and spices and fry for 2 minutes, stirring frequently, until the onion has softened. Add 1 litre of water to the pan along with the pumpkin, salt and pepper.

Bring to the boil and cook, uncovered, for 12 minutes, or until the pumpkin falls apart when poked with a fork. Transfer to a blender and blend until smooth. (You may need to do this in batches.)

Return the soup to the pan over a low heat. Stir through three-quarters of the coconut milk, cover and keep warm.

To make the tofu, heat the oil in a frying pan over a high heat. Add the tofu, sesame seeds, chilli, salt and pepper. Fry for 5 minutes, tossing the tofu occasionally.

Serve the soup topped with the tofu, coriander leaves, spring onion and a swirl of the remaining coconut milk.

SERVES 4–5. GF

RAINBOW VEGGIE PHO

Pho is a Vietnamese soup that is usually made from boiled bones and spices, but this vegan version is un-pho-gettable! (Sorry – I couldn't resist!) This is the perfect soup for replacing electrolytes after a big workout, but if you are watching your sodium intake then halve the amount of miso paste and tamari, as excess salt can be a problem for your blood pressure over a long period of time.

250 g flat rice noodles
1 tablespoon sesame oil
300 g firm tofu, cubed
1 cup sliced shiitake mushrooms (about 150 g),
    leave a couple whole if desired
1 carrot, grated
1 cup shredded cabbage
2 bunches of bok choy (about 800 g), roughly chopped
handful of snow peas (about 100 g), halved
½ red capsicum, sliced
2 cups bean sprouts (about 150 g)
1 spring onion, sliced
2 cups soft herbs (mint, basil and/or coriander)
juice of 1 lime
1 tablespoon sesame seeds

STOCK
1 tablespoon sesame oil
1 onion, diced
4 star anise
8 cloves
½ teaspoon fennel seeds
1 teaspoon ground coriander
2 cinnamon sticks
3 garlic cloves, diced
1 long red chilli, sliced
3 cm piece of ginger, peeled and grated
⅓ cup tamari
2 tablespoons white miso paste
1 tablespoon coconut sugar
3 shiitake mushrooms

To make the stock, heat the sesame oil in a large saucepan or stockpot over a medium–high heat. Add the onion and cook for 1 minute. Add the spices, garlic, chilli and ginger and fry for a further 2–3 minutes, stirring frequently. Add 2.5 litres of water along with the tamari, miso, coconut sugar and mushrooms. Cover and bring to the boil. Reduce the heat to low and allow to gently simmer for 20 minutes.

Meanwhile, cook the rice noodles as per the packet instructions. Drain and divide among large serving bowls.

Heat the sesame oil in a large frying pan over a high heat. Add the tofu and mushrooms and fry for 5 minutes, or until golden all over. Divide equally among the serving bowls.

Arrange the remaining vegetables in the bowls and top with the fresh herbs and a squeeze of lime juice. Pour the hot stock through a strainer over the bowls. Sprinkle with sesame seeds and serve hot.

SERVES 3–4

TIPS
- You may like to keep the strained spices in a jar in the fridge for your next batch of pho.
- Make up a double batch of the stock to freeze for another meal.

GREEN SOUP WITH
POLENTA DIPPERS

At first glance, this soup may look like a big bowl of goo, but it's really delicious and amazingly healthy — like a big hug for your insides. Try it with these polenta dippers for something different. Polenta is made from corn and has a sweet, creamy taste.

2 large potatoes
½ head of broccoli (about 300 g), stem and florets
    roughly chopped
1 zucchini, sliced
1 cup frozen peas
1 teaspoon garlic flakes
2 cups baby spinach leaves (about 100 g)
small handful of mint leaves, plus extra sprigs to serve
½ teaspoon salt
coconut milk and chilli flakes, to serve (optional)

POLENTA DIPPERS
¾ cup (110 g) instant polenta
¼ teaspoon salt, plus extra for baking
1 teaspoon extra-virgin olive oil
1 tablespoon dried thyme

TIP
I hope you don't throw away your broccoli stems — they have a sweeter, more subtle flavour than the florets and are great for soups. You can also slice them finely and cook them as you would any veggie.

To make the polenta dippers, bring 2 cups of water to the boil in a saucepan over a high heat. Slowly pour in the polenta, whisking continuously with a fork. Cook for 2–3 minutes, stirring constantly, until the polenta has a thick, porridge-like consistency. Stir in the salt and remove the pan from the heat.

Line a 20 cm x 10 cm baking tin with baking paper. Pour the polenta mixture into the tray to a thickness of about 1 cm. Place in the fridge to set for 1 hour (or overnight), or in the freezer for 30 minutes.

Preheat the oven to 180°C fan-forced (200°C conventional).

Once the polenta is set, lift it out of the tray and cut it into 2 cm x 8 cm batons. Place them on a baking tray lined with baking paper. Brush with the oil, sprinkle with the thyme and a little extra salt and bake for 30 minutes, or until golden and crispy.

Meanwhile, to prepare the soup, bring 3 cups of water to the boil in a covered saucepan over a high heat. Add the potato and cook, uncovered, for 10 minutes, or until the potato is soft. Add the broccoli, zucchini, peas, and garlic and cook for a further 3–5 minutes. Transfer to a blender with the spinach, mint and salt and blend until smooth.

Serve with a dash of coconut milk, a sprinkle of chilli flakes (if desired), a sprig or two of mint and the dippers on the side. Dunk and enjoy!

SERVES 4, GF

MEDICINAL MUSHROOM SOUP

When you're feeling under the weather, this soup is the perfect remedy. Turmeric contains curcumin, which has proven anti-inflammatory properties; ginger is well known for its anti-nausea effects; and garlic contains allicin, believed to have antibacterial, antifungal and anti-inflammatory properties. But even if you didn't know all that, this soup is just plain delicious.

1 tablespoon sesame oil
5 cm piece of fresh turmeric, grated
5 cm piece of ginger, peeled and grated
1 teaspoon ground cinnamon
½ teaspoon chilli flakes, plus extra to serve (optional)
2 garlic cloves, finely diced
freshly ground black pepper, to taste
1 x 400 ml can full-fat coconut milk
¼ cup tamari
200 g mushrooms (any kind), sliced
200 g cherry tomatoes, halved
100 g sugar snap peas, trimmed
juice of 1 lime
Thai basil leaves, to serve
pinch of ground turmeric, to serve (optional)

Heat the sesame oil in a saucepan over a high heat. Add the turmeric, ginger, cinnamon, chilli, garlic and pepper and fry for 1–2 minutes, or until fragrant. Pour in 1 litre of water and bring to the boil. Reduce the heat to low and stir in the coconut milk, breaking up any solidified bits. When the coconut milk is hot but not boiling, add the tamari, mushrooms, tomatoes and sugar snap peas and cook for 2 minutes.

Remove the pan from the heat and stir in the lime juice. Serve the soup immediately topped with the basil leaves, extra chilli flakes (if using) and a twist of pepper. Finish with a lucky last sprinkle of ground turmeric, if desired.

SERVES 3–4. GF

TIP

Thai basil is a type of basil from South-East Asia that has a subtle anise or liquorice taste. It can usually be found at Asian supermarkets or your local farmers' market. If you can't find any, simply use ordinary basil.

PURPLE SOUP

This is probably the simplest soup you could ever make. White-skinned, purple flesh (WSPF) sweet potato can often be found at your local farmers' market. Although purple sweet potatoes contain slightly less vitamin A than the orange variety, they are believed to have a higher antioxidant content. Sweet potatoes also contain complex carbohydrates for sustained energy and fibre for good gut health.

1 teaspoon extra-virgin olive oil
1 onion, diced
2 garlic cloves, diced
500 g purple sweet potato, scrubbed and cubed
¼ head of cauliflower (about 350 g), chopped
½ teaspoon salt
1 cup frozen peas, thawed
freshly ground black pepper
2 teaspoons sesame seeds
small handful of mint leaves

Heat the oil in a large saucepan over a high heat. Add the onion and garlic and fry for 2 minutes, stirring occasionally, until the onion has softened. Add 1 litre of water to the pan, cover and bring to the boil. Add the sweet potato, reduce the heat to medium and simmer, covered, for 5 minutes. Add the cauliflower and cook for a further 5 minutes.

Drain the water from the pan into a bowl and set it aside.

Transfer the cooked vegetables to a blender. Add the salt and blend until smooth, adding splashes of the reserved water until the soup reaches the desired consistency.

Serve topped with a handful of peas, a twist of freshly ground black pepper, a sprinkle of sesame seeds and a couple of mint leaves.

SERVES 3–4. GF

Eat less
from a box
and more from
the earth

STRAWBERRY, ROCKET
AND BUCKWHEAT SALAD
WITH ALMOND FETA

This is a really fresh summery salad — perfect for picnics, barbecues or even for Christmas day. The strawberries and balsamic vinegar are really tasty together, and the cooked buckwheat adds a contrast in texture. (I often sprinkle raw buckwheat over smoothie bowls or coconut yoghurt to add some crunch, but you don't often see it cooked in dishes. It's softer but still has that delicious nutty taste.)

1 cup buckwheat
⅓ cup balsamic vinegar
1 tablespoon maple syrup
250 g strawberries, hulled and sliced
150 g rocket
½ red onion, finely sliced
150 g Herby Almond Feta (see recipe page 280), sliced
edible flowers, to serve (optional)

TIP
Cook a double batch of buckwheat and store what you don't use for the salad in a container in the fridge. Reheat it with some nut milk and a handful of berries for an alternative to porridge.

Bring 3 cups of water to the boil in a saucepan over a high heat. Add the buckwheat. Cover and cook for 10–12 minutes, or until the buckwheat is soft and fluffy.

Drain the buckwheat and place it in a bowl in the fridge for 20 minutes to cool.

Place the balsamic vinegar and maple syrup in a jar, seal and shake.

Transfer the cooled buckwheat to a large serving bowl. Add the strawberries, rocket, onion and dressing and toss well. Top with the sliced almond feta and edible flowers (if using). Serve as a light main or as a side with some veggie patties or falafel.

SERVES 4 (OR 6 AS A SIDE). GF

BUDDHA BOWLS

Only one in 20 Australians eat the recommended five serves of veggies per day, but this fun recipe is a great way to sneak more serves in. It's got the perfect balance of nutrients, looks amazing and tastes delicious.

¾ cup brown rice
1 purple sweet potato, cubed
400 g pumpkin, deseeded and cut into thick slices
2 teaspoons extra-virgin olive oil
1 teaspoon cumin seeds
pinch of salt
1 bunch of asparagus (about 180 g), woody ends snapped
4–5 zucchini flowers, halved lengthways (optional)
½ cup cherry tomatoes, halved
1 small cucumber, sliced
½ cup alfalfa sprouts
2 cups baby spinach leaves (about 100 g)
1 avocado, sliced
½ cup Beetroot Sauerkraut (see recipe page 332)
½ cup (about 75 g) blueberries
edible flowers (optional)
1 tablespoon sesame seeds
½ cup Traditional Hummus (see recipe page 300)
juice of 1 lemon

Preheat the oven to 180°C fan-forced (200°C conventional).

Cook the rice according to the packet instructions, or use a rice cooker.

Meanwhile, place the sweet potato and pumpkin on a lined baking tray. Brush with the oil and sprinkle over the cumin seeds and salt. Bake for 30 minutes, or until golden and cooked through. In the last 10 minutes, add the asparagus and zucchini flowers (if using).

Roughly mash the sweet potato, divide into four portions and place each portion to one side of four wide, shallow serving bowls. Arrange the roast pumpkin, asparagus, rice and the remaining vegetables and fruit in separate little piles around the bowl. Garnish with the zucchini flowers and edible flowers (if using). Finish with a sprinkle of sesame seeds, a dollop of hummus and a squeeze of lemon juice.

SERVES 4

MIDDLE-EASTERN SALAD
WITH TZATZIKI DRESSING

This is one of those salads that you just can't stop eating. The olives and sultanas give little bursts of saltiness and sweetness that keep you coming back for more. Plus, my homemade vegan tzatziki dressing is super tasty! Cashews give it a creamy texture without the need for dairy. Eating nuts daily has been shown to reduce your risk of heart disease by 30–50 per cent.

1 cup brown rice
1 x 400 g can brown lentils, drained and rinsed
1 small cucumber, cut into matchsticks
1 red capsicum, halved, deseeded and finely sliced
1 teaspoon ground cumin
¼ cup sultanas
½ cup green Sicilian olives
handful of mint leaves

TZATZIKI DRESSING
½ cup cashews, pre-soaked (see page 18)
juice of 1 lemon
½ teaspoon salt
1 garlic clove
1 tablespoon extra-virgin olive oil
1 tablespoon apple cider vinegar
1 tablespoon sesame seeds
¼ cup finely sliced mint leaves
1 small cucumber, cut into matchsticks
1 teaspoon chilli flakes (optional)

Cook the rice according to the packet instructions, or use a rice cooker.

Transfer the cooked rice to a large mixing bowl and set aside for 20 minutes to cool.

When cool, add the lentils, cucumber, capsicum, cumin, sultanas and olives and toss until well combined. Sprinkle over the mint leaves.

To make the tzatziki dressing, place the cashews, lemon juice, salt, garlic, oil, vinegar and sesame seeds in a blender with ½ cup of water. Blend until smooth then transfer to a bowl. Stir in the chopped mint and cucumber and sprinkle with chilli flakes, if desired. Serve the salad topped with a drizzle of tzatziki dressing.

SERVES 4. GF

TIPS
- *This salad keeps well for lunch the next day.*
- *Leftover dressing can be kept in the fridge for up to 4 days. Try drizzling it over roasted vegetables or falafel, or serve it as a dipping sauce for sweet potato chips (see recipe page 314).*

TURMERIC, CAULIFLOWER
AND COUSCOUS SALAD

This salad is packed with nutrients. Wholegrain couscous provides carbohydrates to give you heaps of energy; chickpeas contain fibre, carbs, plant protein, iron and zinc; and cabbage is rich in vitamin C, vitamin K and folate. The chopped dates add a burst of sweetness to the salad, and the creamy turmeric dressing is really scrumptious!

½ head of cauliflower (about 750 g), florets and stems chopped
½ cup wholegrain couscous
1 cup boiling water
1 teaspoon extra-virgin olive oil
1 x 400 g can chickpeas, drained and rinsed
75 g medjool dates (about 4), pitted and sliced
¼ small white cabbage (about 150 g), cored and shredded
100 g kale, stems removed, leaves shredded (about 2 cups)

TURMERIC DRESSING
⅓ cup coconut yoghurt
juice of 1 lemon
1 teaspoon ground turmeric
½ teaspoon freshly ground black pepper
salt, to taste

Bring 1 litre of water to the boil in a saucepan over a high heat. Add the cauliflower and cook, uncovered, for 5–7 minutes, or until the cauliflower is just soft. Drain and set aside to cool slightly.

Meanwhile, place the couscous and boiling water in a bowl. Stir through the oil, cover and allow to sit for 4–5 minutes.

Fluff the couscous with a fork. Transfer to a large bowl with the cauliflower, chickpeas, dates, cabbage and kale and toss together.

To make the dressing, place all the ingredients in a small bowl and stir well.

Serve the salad drizzled with the turmeric dressing. Enjoy!

SERVES 6

GORGEOUS GREEN

PESTO SALAD

This salad celebrates all things green. Green veggies are nutrient powerhouses and contain iron, vitamin A, vitamin C, vitamin K and folate. My fave way to have this is tossed with some wholemeal pasta.

1 teaspoon extra-virgin olive oil
2 cups shredded Tuscan kale (about 200 g)
1 bunch of asparagus (about 180 g), woody ends snapped
2 cups baby spinach leaves (about 100 g)
½ cup chopped green beans
1 cup snow pea sprouts
½ cup frozen peas, thawed
1 cup sliced sugar snap peas
1 zucchini, diced
½ avocado, sliced
½ cup Super Green Pesto (see recipe page 303)
juice of 1 lemon
1 teaspoon pumpkin seeds (optional)

Heat the oil in a frying pan over a medium heat. Add the kale and asparagus and sauté for 3 minutes. Remove the kale and transfer to a serving bowl. Continue cooking the asparagus for a further 2 minutes, turning regularly, until all sides are golden. Transfer to the serving bowl.

Place the spinach, beans, sprouts, peas, sugar snap peas, zucchini and avocado in the bowl. Drizzle over the pesto, squeeze over the lemon juice and sprinkle with the pumpkin seeds (if using). Toss gently before serving.

SERVES 2. GF

SOBA NOODLE SALAD
WITH ROASTED PUMPKIN

This Japanese salad reminds me of evening picnics by the beach. We'd pack it in a cooler bag (it's delicious hot or cold), grab a rug and a couple of forks and head off to watch the sunset. Soba noodles are made from buckwheat flour, which is gluten free, but always read the ingredients list as some contain a mix of buckwheat and wheat flour. Edamame are immature soy beans and are a great source of protein. You can find them in the frozen section of Asian supermarkets and most regular supermarkets.

1 kg kent pumpkin, deseeded and cut into 3 cm wedges
200 g buckwheat soba noodles
160 g edamame, frozen
160 g snow peas, halved
1 spring onion, sliced
2 cups leafy greens (about 100 g) (rocket, cos lettuce,
    baby spinach leaves)
1 cucumber, spiralised into wide ribbons
edible flowers, to serve (optional)

PUMPKIN MARINADE
3 teaspoons sesame oil
1 tablespoon maple syrup
2 teaspoons sesame seeds
1 tablespoon tamari

GINGER-LIME DRESSING
1 tablespoon miso paste
1 tablespoon tamari
1 tablespoon apple cider vinegar
juice of 1 lime
1 tablespoon grated ginger
2 teaspoons maple syrup (optional)
chilli flakes (optional)

Preheat the oven to 180°C fan-forced (200°C conventional). Line a large baking tray with baking paper.

Place all of the pumpkin marinade ingredients in a jar. Secure the lid and shake well.

Arrange the pumpkin pieces over the base of the prepared tray and pour over the marinade. Bake for 45 minutes, or until the pumpkin is soft and golden.

Meanwhile, place all of the dressing ingredients in another jar. Secure the lid, shake well and set aside.

Cook the soba noodles in a saucepan of boiling water as per the packet instructions (approximately 5 minutes). Drain and set aside.

Place the edamame in a bowl and cover with boiling water. Allow them to sit for 30 seconds to thaw. Drain, then squeeze the beans from the pods.

To serve warm, place the pumpkin, soba noodles, edamame, snow peas, spring onion, leafy greens and cucumber in a large serving bowl. Drizzle over the dressing and toss to combine. Serve immediately.

To serve cold, refrigerate the pumpkin, noodles and edamame before tossing with the remaining ingredients. Dress the salad right before serving and sprinkle with edible flowers, if desired.

SERVES 4, GF

POMEGRANATE AND QUINOA
TABOULI

This is a really simple salad but looks quite exciting. The pomegranate seeds add little bursts of colour and sweetness. I've also added quinoa, as it's a complete protein. This means it contains all nine essential amino acids (those which the body cannot produce) that are needed to create all kinds of proteins in the body.

¼ cup tri-colour quinoa, rinsed
2 cups curly parsley, finely chopped
3 tomatoes, diced
seeds of ½ pomegranate (see Tips)
1 tablespoon lemon juice
2 tablespoons extra-virgin olive oil

TIPS

- *To get the seeds out, cut the pomegranate in half and place one half cut side down in a bowl. Now tap the skin firmly with a heavy metal spoon.*
- *If pomegranate is out of season you can swap it for some dried cranberries or fresh diced strawberries.*

Place the quinoa and 1 cup of water in a saucepan over a high heat. Bring to the boil and cook, uncovered, for 10–15 minutes, or until the quinoa is fluffy and has sprouted little tails. Drain. Transfer to a strainer and place over a bowl in the fridge for 20 minutes to cool.

In a serving bowl, toss together the parsley, tomato, pomegranate seeds, lemon juice and oil. Add the cooled quinoa and toss again. Serve in pita pockets with falafel and hummus (see recipes on pages 170 and 300).

SERVES 2 (OR 4 AS A SIDE). GF

CRISPY BAKED POTATO SALAD
WITH CROUTONS

I wanted to share this recipe with you, as it's the one that got me through some of my longest days while juggling uni, a full-time practical placement and writing this book! It was easy to whip up and gave me so much energy.

3 potatoes, cut into chunks
¼ teaspoon salt
1 tablespoon dried rosemary
2 teaspoons extra-virgin olive oil
2 slices rye bread, cut into cubes
1 teaspoon garlic flakes
1 baby cos lettuce, shredded
1 cup cherry or heirloom tomatoes, halved
½ red onion, sliced
1 avocado, sliced
2 tablespoons Beetroot Sauerkraut (see recipe page 332)
1 tablespoon chopped walnuts, pre-soaked (see page 18)
2 tablespoons balsamic vinegar

Preheat the oven to 180°C fan-forced (200°C conventional). Line a baking tray with baking paper.

Place the potato in a saucepan of water and bring to the boil over a high heat. Reduce the heat and cook for 8 minutes, or until just tender. Drain. Add the salt, rosemary and half of the oil. Place a lid on the pan and give the pan 3–5 shakes, so that the potatoes just begin to break up. Transfer the potatoes to the prepared tray and bake for 25 minutes, or until golden and crunchy.

Toss the bread in the remaining oil and the garlic flakes and add to the baking tray 5 minutes before the potatoes are ready.

Divide the salad ingredients among serving plates, drizzle with the balsamic vinegar and top with the crispy baked potatoes and crunchy rye croutons.

SERVES 2–3

VEGGIES ARE THE STARS OF THESE MAGNIFICENT MAINS

RED WINE LENTILS
WITH SWEET POTATO MASH

This hearty lentil stew has been a long-time favourite in my home. I have fond memories of cooking it for my dad's side of the family for Christmas one year. Dad and my brother were hesitant about vegan food (my dad calls it 'rabbit food'), but everyone loved it and there certainly weren't any leftovers! When shopping for red wine, try the organic wine section, as most red wines are technically not vegan because they use 'fining agents' such as casein (milk protein), albumin (from eggs), gelatine (animal protein) and isinglass (fish intestines) to clarify them. Look for a 'vegan friendly' or 'vegan' label on the back.

1 tablespoon extra-virgin olive oil
3 bay leaves
1 tablespoon mustard seeds
2 garlic cloves, finely diced
1 onion, diced
2 x 400 g cans salt-reduced whole peeled tomatoes
2 x 400 g cans brown lentils, drained and rinsed
1 red capsicum, sliced
2 cups sliced button mushrooms (about 200 g)
1 cup organic red wine
salt and freshly ground black pepper
½ cup kalamata olives

SWEET POTATO MASH
2 sweet potatoes, scrubbed and roughly diced
¼ cup Almond Milk (see recipe page 279)
pinch of salt

TO SERVE
1 avocado, sliced (optional)
⅓ cup Cashew Cream Cheese (see recipe page 285)
handful of dill fronds or parsley sprigs
freshly ground black pepper

Heat the oil in a saucepan over a medium–high heat. Add the bay leaves and mustard seeds and sauté for 1 minute until fragrant. Add the garlic and onion and sauté for 2–3 minutes, or until the onion is soft. Stir in the tomatoes (breaking them up with a wooden spoon), lentils, capsicum and mushrooms. Reduce the heat to low and simmer for 10 minutes, uncovered. Pour in the wine and simmer for a further 5 minutes. Season to taste with salt and pepper. Just before serving, add the olives.

Meanwhile, to make the mash, half-fill a saucepan with water and bring to the boil over a high heat. Add the sweet potato and cook, uncovered, for 8–10 minutes, or until the potato breaks apart easily with a fork. Drain and mash in the pan (or transfer to a blender), gradually adding enough of the almond milk to make it creamy and smooth. Season with salt.

Divide the mash among serving bowls. Ladle over the lentil stew and top with sliced avocado (if using), a tablespoon of cashew cream cheese, a sprinkle of fresh herbs and a twist of pepper.

SERVES 4–6, GF

THAI GREEN CURRY

This recipe builds on the delicious Green Curry Paste on page 328. You can use any veggies for this curry, but I love to keep in line with the green theme. Broccolini, a lanky relative of broccoli, is rich in vitamin C, vitamin A and vitamin K. I like my veggies with a bit of crunch, as it helps to keep the nutrients intact.

¾ cup brown rice
1 teaspoon sesame oil
3–4 tablespoons Green Curry Paste (see recipe page 328)
1 teaspoon coconut sugar
1 tablespoon tamari
250 g firm tofu, cubed
1 zucchini, sliced
½ cup bamboo shoots
1 bunch of broccolini (about 175 g), roughly chopped
1 x 400 ml can full-fat coconut milk, or to taste
juice of 1 lime

TO SERVE
1 cup bean sprouts (about 80 g)
½ cup chopped coriander leaves and stems
1 spring onion, sliced

TIP

To mix it up a little, why not try your curry with noodles instead of rice? Simply cook 250 g flat rice noodles according to the packet instructions and follow the rest of the recipe.

Cook the rice according to the packet instructions, or use a rice cooker.

Meanwhile, heat a wok over a medium–high heat. Add the sesame oil and curry paste and fry for 1 minute, or until fragrant. Stir in 1½ cups of water, the coconut sugar and tamari. Bring to the boil, uncovered, then reduce the heat to a low simmer. Add the tofu, zucchini, bamboo shoots and broccolini and simmer, uncovered, for 2 minutes. Stir through half of the coconut milk and taste. If you like a milder flavour, add more coconut milk. Cook for 5 minutes, or until the coconut milk is heated through. Remove the pan from the heat and stir through the lime juice.

Serve the curry hot over rice and top with the bean sprouts, coriander and sliced spring onion.

SERVES 3–4, GF

MOROCCAN CHICKPEA TAGINE
WITH
HASSELBACK POTATOES

This stew is the perfect belly warmer in winter. Cooking tomatoes increases their lycopene content, which is the nutrient that gives tomatoes their bright red colour and also happens to be a powerful antioxidant. And while potatoes are not colourful, they are high in potassium, vitamin C, folate and vitamin B6. Here, they're served hasselback-style – a Swedish technique that makes them crispy and amazing. To eat, you simply tear off the crunchy slices and dip them in the stew. Deeelicious!

6 potatoes, scrubbed
2 teaspoons extra-virgin olive oil
1 teaspoon cumin seeds
salt
1 onion, sliced
1½ teaspoons paprika
2 x 400 g cans salt-reduced whole peeled tomatoes
1 red capsicum, sliced
1 green capsicum, sliced
1 x 400 g can chickpeas, drained and rinsed

Preheat the oven to 200°C fan-forced (220°C conventional).

To prepare the hasselback potatoes, use a sharp knife to make a series of vertical cuts along the length of each potato, each 1–2 mm apart and three-quarters of the way through. Transfer to a baking tray. Brush them with half the oil (or spray with olive oil cooking spray) and sprinkle over the cumin seeds and salt. Bake for 40 minutes, or until browned and crispy.

Meanwhile, heat the remaining teaspoon of oil in a saucepan over a medium–high heat. Add the onion and paprika and sauté for 2–3 minutes, or until the onion has softened. Add the tomatoes (breaking them up with a wooden spoon) and red and green capsicum, cover and bring to the boil for 5 minutes. Add the chickpeas, reduce the heat to low and simmer, uncovered, for 5 minutes. Season to taste with salt.

Ladle the stew into bowls and serve with the potatoes on the side.

SERVES 3–4, GF

DAHL-ISCIOUS

Dahl is an Indian-style soup made from lentils and is one of my go-to dinners, because it's so easy, so tasty and *so* good for you. Lentils are a staple in my diet because they are high in protein, iron and fibre, and they're the quickest legume to cook from scratch. Plus, they are very cheap. I prefer to use split lentils, because they become extra thick when you cook them, which is the texture you want for dahl.

1 cup brown rice

DAHL
1 teaspoon extra-virgin olive oil
1 onion, diced
2 tablespoons mustard seeds
1 teaspoon cumin seeds
1 teaspoon ground turmeric
1 teaspoon garam masala
2 garlic cloves, diced
3 cm piece of ginger, peeled and grated
1 cup split red lentils
2 tomatoes, diced
1 corn cob, kernels stripped
1 cup diced cauliflower (about 100 g)
1 small carrot, grated
½ teaspoon salt

KALE SALAD
1 teaspoon sesame oil
2 teaspoons sesame seeds
1 bunch of kale (about 375 g), stems removed, leaves chopped
¼ cup sultanas
edible flower, to serve (optional)

TO SERVE
1 teaspoon chilli flakes
coconut yoghurt
chopped coriander
lime wedges

Cook the rice according to the packet instructions, or use a rice cooker.

To make the dahl, heat the oil in a large saucepan over a medium–high heat.

Add the onion, spices, garlic and ginger. Fry for 3 minutes, or until the onion has softened and the spices are fragrant. Add the lentils, tomatoes and 2 cups of water. Cover and bring to the boil. Reduce the heat and allow to simmer, uncovered, for 20 minutes, stirring occasionally.

Add the corn kernels, cauliflower, carrot, salt and a further ½–1 cup of water (you want the dahl to be like a thick soup, not too dry). Simmer for a further 6–8 minutes.

To make the kale salad, heat the sesame oil in a frying pan over a medium heat. Add the sesame seeds and kale and sauté for 1–2 minutes, stirring occasionally, until the kale is soft. Transfer to a bowl and sprinkle over the sultanas and edible flowers (if using). Serve the kale salad warm.

To serve, place the rice in a bowl and sprinkle over the chilli flakes. Add a generous ladle of dahl and a scoop of kale salad. Top with the coconut yoghurt and coriander and squeeze over some fresh lime.

SERVES 3–4, GF

CREAMY MAC-NO-CHEESE

There are just so many things to love about this pasta dish. It's not only incredibly easy to make but also really healthy. Plus, the pumpkin and cashews are so creamy and sweet, and the nutritional yeast gives it that cheesy flavour. Cashews are a staple in my pantry. They are high in vitamin E (an antioxidant), magnesium (important for blood pressure regulation) and zinc (which aids immune function and healing), and they don't need as much soaking as other nuts.

400 g pumpkin, roughly diced
1 cup (150 g) cashews, pre-soaked (see page 18)
¼ cup nutritional yeast
1 garlic clove, roughly chopped
½ teaspoon salt
300 g gluten-free macaroni
2 cups baby spinach leaves (about 100 g)
freshly ground black pepper
chilli flakes

TIP

I usually keep the skin on the pumpkin for this recipe, but you can peel it if you prefer.

Bring 1 litre of water to the boil in a saucepan over a high heat. Add the pumpkin, cover and boil for 8 minutes, or until the pumpkin falls apart when pierced with a fork. Drain, reserving the cooking liquid.

Place the pumpkin, cashews, yeast, garlic and salt in a blender and blend until smooth. Add three-quarters of the reserved cooking liquid and pulse to combine. Set aside.

Cook the pasta according to the packet instructions. When al dente, turn off the heat and add the spinach leaves. Drain immediately. Add the pumpkin sauce and stir until the pasta is well coated. Season to taste with the pepper and chilli flakes. Serve immediately.

LENTIL AND MUSHROOM RAGU
WITH ZUCCHETTI

Using spiralised zucchini instead of pasta is an easy way to pack more serves of vegetables into your day. Zucchini is low in calories and high in water and fibre. Lentils, like other legumes, also contain plant-based protein, iron and fibre — all good for your insides.

1 x 400 g can salt-reduced whole peeled tomatoes
160 g cherry tomatoes, halved
1 x 400 g can brown lentils, drained and rinsed
1 cup finely sliced mushrooms (about 80 g)
2 zucchini, spiralised
1 cup basil leaves
salt and freshly ground black pepper
nutritional yeast (optional)

Place the tomatoes in a saucepan over a medium heat. Cover and bring to the boil. Stir in the cherry tomatoes, lentils and mushrooms, breaking up the canned tomatoes with a wooden spoon. Reduce the heat and simmer, uncovered, for a further 5–6 minutes.

To serve, place the zucchetti in bowls and top with the hot tomato and lentil sauce. Sprinkle over the basil leaves, season with salt and pepper and add a big pinch of nutritional yeast flakes, if desired.

SERVES 2–3. GF

CAULIFLOWER AND BUCKWHEAT
VEGGIE PIZZA

Cauliflower is such a versatile vegetable. I love adding it to my pizza bases, along with some buckwheat flour to help hold things together. Despite the name, buckwheat is not wheat. It's not even a grain but the seed of a plant related to rhubarb, which makes it naturally gluten free. Plus, it's high in protein and carbohydrates. My favourite topping is a combo of tomatoes, olives and artichokes, as it reminds me of the pizzas in Italy. But you can top yours with anything you like!

BASE
¼ head of cauliflower (about 350 g), florets and stems
    roughly chopped
pinch of salt
2 garlic cloves, roughly chopped
2 teaspoons dried Italian herbs (basil, oregano, rosemary,
    thyme and/or marjoram)
1 teaspoon extra-virgin olive oil
⅔ cup (90 g) buckwheat flour

TOPPING
¼ cup tomato paste
5 cherry tomatoes, halved
6–8 olives, pitted
¼ cup pickled artichoke, sliced
½ zucchini, peeled lengthways into ribbons

TO SERVE
handful of rocket
2 tablespoons Super Green Pesto (see recipe page 303)
small handful of basil leaves
1 teaspoon balsamic vinegar

Preheat the oven to 170°C fan-forced (190°C conventional). Line a large pizza tray or baking tray with baking paper.

Place the cauliflower, salt, garlic and Italian herbs in a food processor or blender. Process until the mixture resembles fine breadcrumbs.

Transfer the cauliflower mixture to a bowl. Add the oil and flour and knead in the bowl to make a rough dough. Place the dough on the prepared tray and press it out to a thickness of 4–5 mm. Bake for 25 minutes, or until golden and crispy around the edges.

Remove the base from the oven. Spread over the tomato paste and top with the tomatoes, olives, artichoke and zucchini. Return to the oven and bake for a further 10 minutes.

To serve, top the pizza with the rocket, pesto, basil and balsamic vinegar. Slice immediately and enjoy hot.

SERVES 2, GF

People who love to eat are the best kind of people

MEXI-LOADED

SWEET POTATOES

This dish celebrates the goodness of sweet potatoes, and they are *so* good! Especially when they start to caramelise. My favourite type is the white-skinned, purple flesh (WSPF) variety, which has a dense, cakey texture when baked. All sweet potatoes are high in beta-carotene, a precursor for vitamin A. Plus, cumin, sweet potato and black beans all contain iron, which our bodies readily absorb when eaten with vitamin C–rich tomatoes and capsicum.

3 sweet potatoes (any variety), scrubbed
1 teaspoon extra-virgin olive oil
1 teaspoon smoked paprika, plus extra to serve
1 teaspoon ground cumin
1 x 400 g can black beans, drained and rinsed
2 tomatoes, diced
1 red capsicum, diced
½ corn cob, kernels stripped
½ cup finely shredded red cabbage
1 avocado mashed with the juice of 1 lime
¼ cup coriander leaves
¼ cup Cashew Cream Cheese (see recipe page 285)
1 teaspoon habañero chilli sauce, or other chilli sauce
1 jalapeño, sliced, to serve (optional)

Preheat the oven to 170°C fan-forced (190°C conventional).

Place the sweet potatoes on a baking tray and bake for 45 minutes, or until easily pierced with a fork.

Meanwhile, heat the oil in a saucepan over a medium heat. Add the paprika and cumin and fry for 1 minute until fragrant. Add the black beans, tomato and capsicum. Reduce the heat to low and simmer for 6–8 minutes, or until the capsicum is soft and the tomato juices have thickened.

Heat a frying pan over a medium heat. Add the corn and fry for 2 minutes, or until browned. Remove from the heat and set aside.

When the potatoes are ready, cut them open lengthways and fill with the bean mixture. To serve, top each with the cabbage, corn, avocado, coriander, cashew cream, chilli sauce and sliced jalapeño (if using). Finish with an extra sprinkle of smoked paprika.

SERVES 3, GF

EGGPLANT CANNELLONI

These eggplant cannelloni are a great grain-free substitute for pasta. I like using vegetables instead of pasta for my evening meal, because I often go straight to bed after dinner – there's no point loading myself up with grain-based carbs if I'm not going to be using the energy. Eggplants are high in fibre, which means they're great for getting your digestive system moving. This meal reminds me of my travels to Greece, where we ate loads of zucchini and eggplant in rich tomato sauces. Yum!

¼ small head of cauliflower (about 300 g), roughly chopped
1 large eggplant, sliced lengthways into 3 mm thick slices
   (reserve the small offcuts for the sauce)
1 large zucchini, sliced lengthways into 2 mm thick slices
   (reserve the small offcuts for the sauce)
½ cup cashews, pre-soaked (see page 18)
1 tablespoon nutritional yeast
pinch of ground nutmeg
1 cup baby spinach leaves (about 50 g), finely chopped
handful of basil leaves, finely chopped, plus extra leaves to serve
1 x 400 g can diced tomatoes
salt and freshly ground black pepper

Preheat the oven to 180°C fan-forced (200°C conventional).

Start with the sauce. Bring 1 litre of water to the boil in a saucepan over a high heat. Add the cauliflower and the offcuts of eggplant and zucchini and cook for 5 minutes, or until tender. Drain. Transfer to a food processor or blender with the cashews, yeast and nutmeg. Process until smooth. Stir through the spinach and basil and set aside.

Heat a large frying pan over a medium–high heat. Place the eggplant and zucchini slices in the pan and fry (no oil) for 1–2 minutes on each side, or until golden and floppy. Set aside.

Pour the tomatoes into the base of a baking dish and season with salt and pepper.

On a clean work surface, place a slice of zucchini. Arrange an eggplant slice lengthways and centred over the zucchini. Spoon a heaped tablespoon of the cauliflower mixture in the centre of the eggplant slice. Roll up the zucchini and eggplant to form a tube. Place in the tomato sauce with the loose end facing down. Repeat with the remaining zucchini, eggplant and filling.

Bake the cannelloni for 40–45 minutes, or until the tomato sauce has bubbled and reduced and the cannelloni rolls are golden. Scatter over a couple of extra basil leaves and serve with a side salad.

SERVES 2–3. GF

CRISPY JALAPEÑO-INFUSED
CAULIFLOWER TACOS

Alex is obsessed with all things Mexican, so I am constantly experimenting with different ways to jazz up tacos. This one is a beauty! The black beans provide the all-important protein and iron, and I love the hint of smokiness and spice in the jalapeño battered cauliflower. If you don't like kiwifruit for the salsa, simply use mango instead – it's just as yummy.

CRISPY CAULIFLOWER
1 cup (160 g) wholemeal plain flour
1 cup soy milk or other non-dairy milk (see recipes page 279)
¼ cup sliced pickled jalapeños
2 teaspoons smoked paprika
1 teaspoon extra-virgin olive oil
½ teaspoon salt
¾ head of cauliflower (about 1 kg), cut into florets

SLAW
2 carrots, grated or cut into matchsticks
¼ red cabbage (about 150 g), shredded
½ cup coconut yoghurt
1 tablespoon apple cider vinegar

KIWI SALSA
2 kiwifruit, skin removed
juice of ½ lime
2 teaspoons habañero chilli sauce, or any chilli sauce

TO SERVE
12 soft wholemeal tortillas
1 x 400 g can black beans, drained and rinsed
250 g cherry tomatoes, quartered
2 limes, halved
habañero chilli sauce, or other chilli sauce
smashed avocado (optional)
sliced green or red chilli (optional)

Preheat the oven to 170°C fan-forced (190°C conventional). Line two baking trays with baking paper.

To make the crispy cauliflower, place the flour, milk, jalapeño, paprika, oil and salt in a blender and blend until smooth. Pour into a bowl. Dunk the head of each cauliflower floret into the batter, shaking off the excess. Place on the baking trays, ensuring the florets aren't touching. Bake for 40 minutes, or until browned and crispy.

Meanwhile, prepare the slaw by combining all the ingredients in a mixing bowl. Cover and place in the fridge.

To make the kiwi salsa, place all the ingredients in a blender and blitz until smooth. Pour into a bowl and set aside.

To serve, place everything on plates or in bowls, and let everyone assemble their own tacos.

SERVES 4-6

TIP
I use a julienne peeler to cut my carrots into little matchsticks, but you can also use a sharp knife or a mandoline with a julienne attachment.

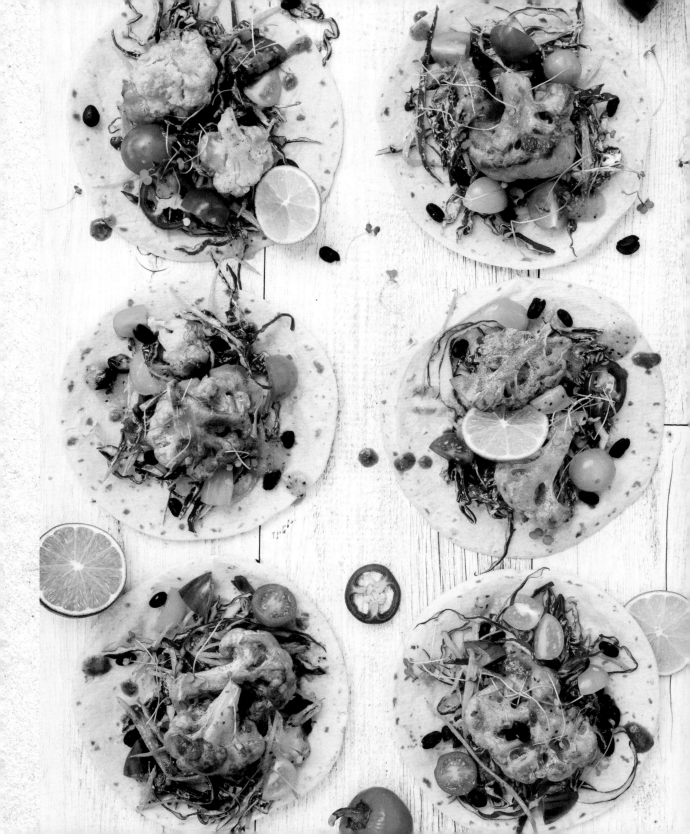

SUSHI BOWLS

Japanese food really interests me, as it's one of the healthiest cuisines in the world. I really enjoy cooking with Japanese ingredients, such as rice, tofu, seaweed and pickled ginger. This is the perfect meal when you feel like sushi but don't have the time to make fiddly nori rolls. Adding vinegar and nut butter to the rice helps it to stick together and makes it really tasty.

1 cup brown rice
2 tablespoons rice vinegar
1 tablespoon nut butter (any kind)
2 teaspoons sesame oil
250 g firm tofu or tempeh (or both), cubed or sliced into batons
1 cup sliced shiitake mushrooms
2 tablespoons sesame seeds
¼ cup tamari
8 cos lettuce leaves
1 carrot, cut into matchsticks
1 cup shredded red cabbage
1 cucumber, peeled lengthways into ribbons
1 avocado, diced
¼ cup pickled ginger
¼ cup Cashew Cream Cheese (see recipe page 285)
4 nori sheets, shredded
1 lime, cut into wedges

Cook the rice according to the packet instructions. Drain well. Stir in the vinegar and nut butter and set aside.

Heat the oil in a large frying pan over a medium heat. Add the tofu and/or tempeh and fry on each side for 2–3 minutes, or until golden. Remove from the pan, then add the mushrooms and sesame seeds to the same pan and stir-fry for 3 minutes, or until golden.

Divide the rice among four bowls and top with the fried tofu and/or tempeh and the mushrooms. Add a splash of tamari, nestle two lettuce leaves on the side of each bowl, then arrange a quarter each of the carrot, cabbage, rolled cucumber ribbons, avocado and pickled ginger on top. Dab on a tablespoon of cream cheese (or use an icing bag to pipe it on) and top with the shredded nori and lime wedges. Eat as you would a salad or challenge yourself with a pair of chopsticks.

SERVES 4. GF

SATAY PINEAPPLE

FRIED RICE

This dish is the perfect example of what it means to 'eat a rainbow' – it's brimming with gorgeous coloured veggies and fruit, as well as seeds, peanuts and tofu. I always use brown rice, as it's higher in fibre and has a lower GI than white rice, which means you'll feel satisfied for longer. Plus, I love the nutty flavour and texture. And the satay sauce … well, let's just say it's addictive. Make up a batch by itself to pour over steamed veggies, or use it as a dipping sauce for rice paper rolls.

1 cup brown rice
1 tablespoon sesame oil
250 g firm tofu, cubed
2 teaspoons sesame seeds
1 long red chilli, sliced
salt and freshly ground black pepper
1 cup shredded red cabbage
½ red capsicum, sliced
1 spring onion, sliced
1 carrot, cut into matchsticks
1 bunch of bok choy (about 400 g), chopped
½ cup frozen peas
1 cup chopped fresh pineapple (or cut into stars using
    a cookie cutter)
2 tablespoons roasted unsalted peanuts
2 tablespoons tamari
1 cup (80 g) bean sprouts

SATAY SAUCE
½ cup Peanut Sesame Butter (see recipe page 286)
    or natural peanut butter (see Tip page 286)
juice of 1 lime
2 tablespoons tamari
1 tablespoon sesame oil

Cook the rice according to the packet instructions, or use a rice cooker. Set aside.

To make the satay sauce, place all of the ingredients in a jar with ⅓ cup of water. Seal and shake vigorously. Set aside.

Heat the sesame oil in a large frying pan or wok over a high heat. Add the tofu, sesame seeds, chilli and salt and pepper. Fry for 5–6 minutes, tossing the tofu occasionally to brown on all sides. Transfer to a bowl and set aside.

In the same pan or wok, place the cabbage, capsicum, spring onion, carrot, bok choy, peas and pineapple. Stir-fry for 2 minutes. Add the cooked rice, peanuts and tamari and toss together. Stir-fry for another 3 minutes.

Serve the fried rice topped with the tofu, bean sprouts and a drizzle of satay sauce.

SERVES 3–4, GF

MOROCCAN-INSPIRED
VEGGIE PATTIES

These veggie patties make great burgers (see recipe page 168), but they're also delicious hot or cold with a salad. The lentils and quinoa provide a complete source of plant-based protein, as well as a decent amount of iron — two of the key nutrients for those on a vegan diet.

1 large sweet potato (about 500 g), cut into 2 cm cubes
½ cup quinoa, rinsed
½ cup red lentils
½ cup grated carrot
¼ cup diced dried apricots
2 garlic cloves, diced
2 teaspoons ground cumin
1 teaspoon mustard seeds
½ teaspoon ground cinnamon
pinch of salt
¼ cup sesame seeds
1 spring onion, sliced, to serve

Preheat the oven to 180°C fan-forced (200°C conventional) and line a baking tray with baking paper.

Place the sweet potato in a saucepan and cover with water. Bring to the boil over a high heat and cook for 8–10 minutes, or until the sweet potato falls apart when poked with a fork. Drain, transfer to a mixing bowl and set aside.

In the same pan, combine the quinoa and lentils with 2 cups of water. Bring to the boil over a medium heat and cook for 12–15 minutes, or until all the water has been absorbed and the mixture resembles a thick paste. Transfer to the bowl with the sweet potato. Add the carrot, apricot, garlic, cumin, mustard seeds, cinnamon and salt and mash roughly with a fork.

Form the mixture into eight patties and place on the baking tray. Sprinkle the patties with the sesame seeds. Bake for 45–60 minutes, or until the sesame seeds are golden and the patties are firm to touch.

Sprinkle over the spring onion and serve with a side salad or sauerkraut, or in a burger (see page 168).

MAKES 8, GF

TIP
You can store leftover patties in the fridge for up to 4 days (or the freezer for longer!), and reheat them to make your burger on page 168.

MIGHTY VEGAN BURGER TOWER
WITH
KETCHUP AND MAYO

This delicious burger includes the veggie patties on page 164 served with fresh sourdough rolls and my homemade ketchup and cauli mayo. I guarantee you'll have sauce dripping down your arms and a belly full of goodness. Tip: you may need to cut your burger in half!

4 Moroccan-inspired Veggie Patties (see recipe page 164),
    pre-cooked
4 pineapple rings (fresh or canned)
4 sourdough rolls, halved
80 g baby spinach leaves
1 tomato, sliced
½ red onion, sliced
1 avocado, sliced

TOMATO KETCHUP
1–2 ripe tomatoes, finely diced (about 300 g)
¼ red capsicum, diced
2 teaspoons apple cider vinegar
¼ teaspoon salt

CAULIFLOWER MAYO
¼ head of cauliflower (about 350 g), florets and stalks chopped
½ cup cashews, pre-soaked (see page 18)
1 tablespoon apple cider vinegar
1 teaspoon garlic flakes
1 tablespoon nutritional yeast
½ teaspoon salt

To make the ketchup, place all the ingredients in a saucepan, cover and bring to the boil over a medium heat. Remove the lid and simmer for 8 minutes, or until the sauce has thickened. If you like your ketchup smooth, transfer the mixture to a blender and blitz until smooth. Pour the ketchup into a bowl and place in the fridge to cool for 30 minutes.

To make the mayo, half-fill a saucepan with water and bring to the boil over a high heat. Add the cauliflower florets and cook for 8 minutes, or until soft. Drain and transfer to a blender or food processor along with the remaining mayo ingredients. Blend until smooth. Transfer to a bowl and place in the fridge to cool.

Meanwhile, to reheat the veggie patties, place them in a frying pan over a medium heat for 5 minutes, or until heated through. (Or place them on a baking tray in a preheated 160°C oven for 15 minutes.) Transfer to a warmed serving plate.

Heat a frying pan over a medium heat. Add the pineapple rings and fry for 2 minutes on each side. Transfer to a serving plate.

To serve, place the rolls, spinach, tomato, onion and avocado on serving plates in the centre of the table, along with the warm patties, cooked pineapple and bowls of sauce. Everyone then constructs their own burger and tucks in!

SERVES 4 HUNGRY PEOPLE

GREEN PEA FALAFEL

Falafel are Middle Eastern mini patties made from spiced, deep-fried chickpeas. I've given mine a healthy twist by including green peas and baking them instead of frying them in oil. Chickpeas are a great source of plant protein and fibre, so they are an excellent way to bulk up your meal and add some crunchy texture. These are great served as part of a mezze board (see recipe on page 175).

2 cups frozen peas, thawed
1 x 400 g can chickpeas, drained and rinsed
½ teaspoon salt
1 teaspoon ground cumin
1 teaspoon garlic flakes
1 cup chopped fresh herbs (mint, parsley, coriander)
½ cup (75 g) buckwheat flour, sifted
1 teaspoon extra-virgin olive oil
2 tablespoons sesame seeds

Preheat the oven to 180°C fan-forced (200°C conventional) and line a baking tray with baking paper.

Place the peas, chickpeas, salt, cumin, garlic flakes and herbs in a food processor or blender. Pulse to a thick green paste – some chunky bits are fine.

Transfer the mixture to a bowl and fold in the flour. If the mixture is too sticky, add 1–2 teaspoons of flour until you have a dough-like consistency. Roll heaped tablespoons of the mixture into balls and place on the prepared tray. Brush with the oil and sprinkle with the sesame seeds. Bake for 25–30 minutes, or until golden and crispy.

Serve warm in a wrap with salad and hummus or as part of a mezze board.

MAKES ABOUT 12. GF

FALAFEL MEZZE BOARD

Mezze comes from the Persian word for 'taste' or 'snack' and usually involves lots of small dishes served as a starter or as a main meal. Arranging all of the ingredients in the centre of a large board allows everyone to build their own pita pocket or falafel salad. It's the perfect meal with some afternoon drinks. And eating it with your hands is *totally* okay!

4 large wholemeal pita pockets, cut in half
12 Green Pea Falafel (see recipe page 170)
1½ cups Traditional Hummus (see recipe page 300)
2 cups Pomegranate and Quinoa Tabouli (see recipe page 127)
¾ cup mixed olives
½ cup sauerkraut, store-bought or homemade
 (see recipe page 332)
3 cups shredded cos lettuce
1 jalapeño, sliced

Preheat the oven to 150°C fan-forced (170°C conventional).

Place the pita bread on a baking tray and warm in the oven for 5 minutes.

Arrange all of the ingredients on a large platter. Provide guests with serving plates and allow them to help themselves.

SERVES 4–6

POPEYE PIE

This delicious, dairy-free spanakopita is *so* good for you and is the ultimate vegan comfort meal. Yep, vegans don't just eat lettuce, they eat pies too! This one is chock-full of iron-rich spinach, and the nutritional yeast is even fortified with vitamin B12. Lots of store-bought puff pastry sheets are vegan (using margarine instead of butter) – just make sure to read the ingredients list.

⅓ head of cauliflower (about 500 g), roughly chopped
½ cup cashews, pre-soaked (see page 18)
1 tablespoon nutritional yeast
¼ teaspoon salt
¼ teaspoon ground nutmeg
1 teaspoon extra-virgin olive oil
1 onion, diced
2 garlic cloves, diced
200 g spinach, roughly chopped
2 sheets puff pastry
1 tablespoon pine nuts

Preheat the oven to 170°C fan-forced (190°C conventional).

Bring a saucepan half-filled with water to the boil over a high heat. Add the cauliflower and boil for 7 minutes, or until tender. Drain and transfer to a blender with the cashews, nutritional yeast, salt and nutmeg. Blend until smooth and thick.

Heat the oil in a large frying pan over a medium heat. Add the onion and sauté for 3 minutes, or until softened. Stir in the garlic and sauté for a further 2 minutes. Add the spinach and toss for 15 seconds until wilted.

Remove the pan from the heat and stir in the cauliflower mixture.

Line the base of a 20 cm x 30 cm or 25 cm round pie dish with one sheet of pastry, cutting off any excess that extends over the rim of the dish.

Scoop the spinach and cauliflower mixture onto the pastry, spreading it evenly over the base. Sprinkle over the pine nuts, then lay the remaining pastry sheet over the top, again cutting off any excess. Seal the edges of the pastry by pressing with a fork. If you like, you can decorate the top with the offcuts, using cookie cutters to make little shapes or creating pastry plaits. Bake for 40–45 minutes, or until puffy and golden all over.

Remove the pie from the oven and allow to rest for 5 minutes before slicing and serving with a side salad.

SERVES 4–5

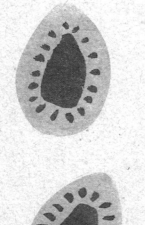

LIFE
IS
SHORT

EAT
DESSERT
FIRST

CARAMEL BALLS

Alex and I made these balls to sell at our local fruit shop, where I worked every Sunday throughout my uni studies. They became so popular that people would call up the shop asking to place bulk orders! I would always tell anyone who asked for the recipe that it was a secret, but now that I can't make them for the shop anymore, I thought it's only fair to share the recipe with the world. The secret to that perfect caramel flavour and crunchy texture is the caramelised buckini cluster granola we mix through, which I buy from my local bulk wholefood store. Alternatively, you could use my Spiced Maple-roasted Granola, omitting the orange zest (see recipe page 48).

2 cups unsalted, roasted cashews
1 cup coconut flakes
½ cup Gooey Caramel Paste (see recipe page 288)
½ teaspoon salt
2 cups gluten-free caramelised buckini clusters
½ cup desiccated coconut

Line a baking tray with baking paper.

Place the cashews and coconut flakes in a food processor or blender and blitz to a fine crumb. Transfer to a mixing bowl with the caramel paste, salt and buckini clusters (crumble some of the bigger chunks). Mix well with your hands to form a thick, sticky mixture. Wash and dry your hands.

Place the desiccated coconut in a shallow bowl for rolling. Form heaped tablespoons of the mixture into 12 balls (about 50 g each). Roll each ball in the coconut and place on the prepared tray. Freeze for 2–4 hours, or until set.

These are delicious eaten straight from the freezer or fridge. They store well in a sealed container in the freezer for 3 weeks, or in the fridge for 7 days – if they last that long!

MAKES 12. GF

JAMMIN' DROPS

Jam drops are a classic and my favourite biscuit ever! I love how crunchy and crumbly these ones are. Plus, they're fun to make. The jam from the Basics chapter is perfect for this recipe, as it turns to a sticky toffee texture when baked. Enjoy these dunked in your morning or afternoon cuppa.

1 cup (160 g) wholemeal plain flour
1 teaspoon baking powder
1 teaspoon vanilla powder
pinch of salt
¼ cup coconut sugar
¼ cup extra-virgin olive oil
1 teaspoon chia seeds
¼ cup Almond Milk (see recipe page 279)
¼ cup Berry Nice Jam (see recipe page 292)

Preheat the oven to 160°C fan-forced (180°C conventional) and line a baking tray with baking paper.

Sift the flour, baking powder, vanilla powder and salt into a mixing bowl and make a well in the centre.

In another bowl, place the coconut sugar, oil, chia seeds and almond milk and mix to combine.

Pour the wet ingredients into the dry ingredients and stir until a rough dough forms. Knead lightly in the bowl and divide into eight even portions. Roll each piece into a ball and place on the prepared tray 2 cm apart.

Use your thumb to press a 1 cm deep hole in the centre of each ball. Fill with 1 teaspoon of jam. Bake for 15–20 minutes, or until golden. Remove from the oven and allow to cool for 15 minutes before turning out onto a wire rack. Enjoy them warm dunked in tea or store them in an airtight container in the fridge for up to 1 week.

MAKES 8

BANANA POPS

I love choc-dipped bananas because they remind me of road trips down south, where we'd stop in at the Big Banana at Coffs Harbour and get one. Make sure you use ripe bananas, as they're a lot sweeter. I've suggested a range of toppings here, but feel free to be as creative as you want.

4 bananas, peeled and halved
8 ice-cream sticks
1 cup Raw Chocolate Sauce (see recipe page 295)
1–2 tablespoons puffed quinoa
1–2 tablespoons chopped nuts
1–2 tablespoons shredded coconut
1–2 tablespoons vegan caramel chocolate (see Tip)
1–2 tablespoons cacao nibs
1–2 teaspoons edible rose petals
1–2 teaspoons coffee beans

TIPS

• *Vegan caramel chocolate contains cacao butter but no cacao powder. It's light brown in colour and can be found at bulk wholefood and health-food stores. If you can't find any, just use any vegan chocolate or increase the quantity of raw chocolate sauce.*
• *Try this recipe using strawberries or watermelon chunks instead of bananas. Both taste delicious dipped in my raw choc!*

Line a baking tray with baking paper.

Insert the ice-cream sticks into the banana halves.

Place the chocolate sauce in a cup or mug and the toppings in little bowls.

Dunk each banana in the chocolate sauce, then sprinkle with one or two different toppings, changing the combination of flavours each time. Place on the prepared tray and freeze for 30–60 minutes, or until the chocolate has set. Leave for 2–3 hours if you would like frozen bananas.

Enjoy straight from the freezer! They'll last well in an airtight container for up to 2 weeks.

MAKES 8, GF

PEPPERMINT CREAM BITES

These little morsels are the perfect bite-sized snack to munch on after tea. I've suggested using silicone ice-cube trays or chocolate moulds, as it's so much easier to remove them, but you could also use mini silicone muffin trays and make them flat and wide like a store-bought peppermint cream.

1½ cups cashews, pre-soaked (see page 18)
½ cup desiccated coconut
⅓ cup coconut milk
1 tablespoon maple syrup
1 teaspoon peppermint extract
1 cup Raw Chocolate Sauce (see recipe page 295)

Place the cashews, coconut, coconut milk, maple syrup and peppermint extract in a blender and blend for 2–4 minutes, or until the mixture forms a smooth paste. Press the mixture into silicone ice-cube trays or mini muffin trays. Place the trays in the freezer to set for 4–6 hours, or overnight.

Remove the bites from the silicone tray and place on a plate. Drizzle 1–2 teaspoons of raw chocolate sauce over each one and return to the freezer for 30 minutes to set. Serve straight from the freezer. These store well in an airtight container in the freezer for up to 4 weeks.

MAKES 12–24. GF

TIP

Instead of peppermint extract you can use peppermint essential oil. Ask for food-grade quality oil at the health-food store. The oil is much stronger than the extract, so you will only need a quarter of the amount (¼ teaspoon). Start with less and add to taste. Peppermint essential oil is a really handy thing to have at home. You can use it to make your own herbal toothpaste or rub it on your temples to make you feel calm. Peppermint is also great when you're feeling a bit nauseous, as it soothes the gastric lining of your tummy and may help reduce muscle spasms in your intestines.

BAKED CUSTARD TARTS

Alex, is obsessed with custard tarts, so I was determined to create a vegan version. I've used cornflour to thicken the milk mixture and flavoured it with vanilla and nutmeg, similar to the custard tarts you find in many Aussie bakeries. The turmeric is really only for colour but has a very strong flavour, so make it the tiniest pinch or use a saffron thread instead. The agar-agar helps to firm up the custard, but you can leave it out if you like.

½ cup (80 g) wholemeal spelt flour
pinch of salt
1 tablespoon extra-virgin olive oil

CUSTARD
1 cup soy milk
2 tablespoons cornflour
1 teaspoon agar-agar (optional)
¼ cup maple syrup
½ teaspoon vanilla powder
½ teaspoon ground nutmeg
tiny pinch of ground turmeric or 1 saffron thread (optional)

Preheat the oven to 170°C fan-forced (190°C conventional). Lightly grease four mini loose-bottomed tart tins.

To make the pastry, sift the flour and salt into a mixing bowl. Make a little well in the centre and pour in ¼ cup of water and the oil. Stir until a soft dough forms. Knead lightly in the bowl and divide into four equal portions.

Place the dough portions on a clean, lightly floured surface. Using a rolling pin or glass bottle, roll out each one into a 4 mm thick circle and press into the prepared tart tins.

Bake for 10 minutes, or until golden and firm. Remove from the oven and set aside.

Reduce the oven to 160°C (180°C).

To make the custard, heat the soy milk in a saucepan over a medium heat. Slowly sprinkle in the cornflour and agar-agar (if using), whisking continuously. Continue whisking until the milk starts to steam, making sure it does not boil. Reduce the heat to low. Add 2 tablespoons of the maple syrup, the vanilla, half of the nutmeg and the turmeric or saffron (if using). Continue stirring until the custard starts to thicken.

Pour the custard into the pastry shells and sprinkle over the remaining nutmeg. Allow to rest for 5 minutes.

Place the tarts on a baking tray and drizzle over the remaining tablespoon of maple syrup. Bake for 10–15 minutes, or until golden on top. Eat warm or store in the fridge for up to 4 days.

MAKES 4

GOLDEN HAPPY-TIMES

These are my take on Golden Gaytimes, and they are absolutely flippin' delicious! Cashews are the secret to getting vegan ice cream smooth and creamy. They also happen to be high in vitamin K, magnesium and zinc.

1 cup cashews, pre-soaked (see page 18)
1 x 400 ml can full-fat coconut milk
90 g medjool dates (about 5), pitted
1 tablespoon coconut oil
1 teaspoon tapioca starch (arrowroot) (optional)
pinch of salt
⅓ cup Gooey Caramel Paste (see recipe page 288)
8 ice-cream sticks
1 cup Raw Chocolate Sauce (see recipe page 295)
½ cup puffed quinoa

Place the cashews, coconut milk, dates, coconut oil, tapioca and salt in a blender and blend until smooth.

Pour the mixture into eight ice-cream moulds until half-filled. Add a heaped teaspoon of caramel paste, then fill the remaining space with the mixture. Insert the ice-cream sticks. Place the moulds in the freezer for 8 hours, or overnight.

Make a batch of raw chocolate sauce and pour it into a glass. Place the puffed quinoa on a plate.

Remove the ice creams from the freezer and pull them out of their moulds (see Tip). Dip each one in the raw chocolate (or spoon it over), then quickly roll in the puffed quinoa. Place in an airtight container and return to the freezer. They'll last for up to 4 weeks if you don't eat them all first!

MAKES 8, GF

TIP

To remove the ice creams from their moulds, slide a small, sharp knife down the inner edge of the moulds and run the outsides very briefly under a little warm water.

I've been refining this recipe for years now, and I think you're going to love it. Cherries are not only bright and bursting with flavour but also high in vitamin C, which (among other things) plays a role in the production of collagen for healthy skin, cartilage, tendons and blood vessels. I've used frozen, pitted cherries but feel free to use fresh ones if they're in season — just don't forget you have to pit them! Alternatively, you can use raspberries or strawberries instead.

3 cups shredded coconut, plus extra to serve
1½ cups frozen, pitted cherries
¼ cup dried cranberries
1 tablespoon coconut oil
1 cup Raw Chocolate Sauce (see recipe page 295),
    or 100 g dark chocolate, melted
handful of fresh cherries, to serve (optional)

Line a 10 cm x 15 cm loaf tin with plastic wrap and set aside.

Place the coconut in a food processor or blender and blitz to a desiccated consistency. Add the frozen cherries and process until the cherries have broken down (some small chunks of cherry are okay). Transfer to a mixing bowl.

Place the cranberries in the food processor and blitz into fine pieces. Tip into the mixing bowl.

Add the coconut oil to the mixing bowl and mix well with your hands. Press the mixture firmly into the base of the prepared tin. Freeze for 4–6 hours, or overnight.

Carefully lift the slice from the tin using the plastic wrap. Cut into eight bars and transfer to a wire rack. Spoon the chocolate sauce over the top to cover each bar, then sprinkle with a little extra coconut. Freeze for 30–60 minutes, or until the chocolate has set. Eat straight from the freezer. If serving as a dessert at a dinner party, pop a few fresh cherries on top to decorate.

Store in an airtight container in the freezer for up to 4 weeks.

MAKES 8. GF

CARAMEL POPCORN
ICE CREAM CONES

For months, I'd been trying to make the perfect vegan ice cream. Yep. Lots of failed recipe attempts (and lots of grainy, icy, bland ice creams). And then it happened: I added some cashews and created a delicious, smooth and creamy vegan ice cream. Serving it in vegan waffle cones with chocolate and popcorn is so much fun.

2 cups cashews, pre-soaked (see page 18)
55 g medjool dates (about 3), pitted
1 x 400 ml can full-fat coconut cream
1 tablespoon coconut oil
¼ teaspoon salt
¼ cup Gooey Caramel Paste (see recipe page 288)
½ cup Raw Chocolate Sauce (see recipe page 295),
    or 50 g vegan dark chocolate, melted
5–6 vegan waffle cones
2 cups lightly salted popcorn (see Tip)

TIP

If popping your own corn, place 2 tablespoons of kernels in a paper bag, seal it and microwave on high for 90 seconds, or until the popping begins to slow. Toss with salt to taste. To cook popcorn on the stovetop, heat a saucepan over a medium heat. Add 1 tablespoon of oil, drop in 2–3 kernels, cover and wait for them to pop. Once the kernels have popped, add 2 tablespoons of kernels. Cover and allow to pop for 30–60 seconds, or until the popping slows. Add salt to taste.

Place the cashews, dates, coconut cream, oil and salt in a blender or food processor. Process for 3 minutes, or until super smooth. Pour into a 10 cm x 15 cm loaf tin. Add the caramel paste, 1 tablespoon at a time, swirling it through lightly. Place in the freezer for 3–4 hours to set.

Place the chocolate sauce or melted chocolate in a shallow bowl. Dip the tops of the waffle cones in the melted chocolate sauce, then sprinkle with most of the popcorn. Place on a baking tray in the fridge for 30 minutes to set.

When the ice cream has set, remove from the freezer and leave on the bench for 5 minutes to soften. Remove the waffle cones from the fridge. Spoon a large scoop of ice cream into each cone and sprinkle with the remaining popcorn. Eat right away.

SERVES 5–6

CHUNKY WHOLESOME
ROCKY ROAD

This chunky rocky road is packed with the goodness of nuts, fruit, grains and coconut. As there are fresh fruits in this recipe, it's best stored in the fridge and should be eaten within a few days. Cherries being a summer stone fruit, I think this makes a great treat to share at Christmas!

170 g vegan dark chocolate, chopped
½ cup puffed rice
¼ cup shelled unsalted pistachios
¼ cup cashews, pre-soaked (see page 18)
½ cup shredded coconut
¼ cup dried cranberries
5–6 cherries
½ cup fresh berries (blueberries and/or raspberries)

TIP
When buying dark chocolate, always read the ingredients list. Avoid those that include milk solids, milk powder or whey in the list.

Line the base and sides of a 30 cm x 20 cm lamington or brownie tin with baking paper.

Melt the chocolate in a heatproof bowl over a saucepan of simmering water.

Combine the puffed rice, nuts, coconut and cranberries in a mixing bowl.
Pour in the melted chocolate, reserving 2 tablespoons, and stir well with a metal spoon (so the chocolate doesn't seize). Transfer the mixture to the prepared tin. Top with the cherries and berries and drizzle over the remaining chocolate. Place in the fridge to set for 1 hour.

Slice the rocky road and serve. Leftovers can be stored in an airtight container in the fridge for up to 3 days.

SERVES 8–10, GF

Start ♡
each day
with a
grateful
heart

FLOURLESS BLACK BEAN
FUDGE BROWNIES

These brownies are completely flourless, really moist and *full* of nutrients. The black beans contain good amounts of plant protein and iron, and the sweet potato provides vitamin A and more iron. There are actually ten serves of veggies in this brownie mix. And it's a dessert! Always keep the skin of your sweet potato on – it contains insoluble fibre (for intestinal health) and heaps of nutrients.

500 g sweet potato, cubed
1 x 400 g can black beans, drained and rinsed
125 g medjool dates (about 7), pitted
½ cup cacao powder
¾ cup Almond Milk (see recipe page 279)
2 tablespoons extra-virgin olive oil
pinch of salt
½ cup Raw Chocolate Sauce (see recipe page 295)
1 cup fresh raspberries
handful of dehydrated edible rose petals

Preheat the oven to 170°C fan-forced (190°C conventional). Line a 20 cm square cake tin or baking dish with baking paper.

Half-fill a saucepan with water and bring to the boil over a high heat. Add the sweet potato and cook for 8 minutes, or until soft. Drain and transfer to a blender with the black beans, dates, cacao powder, almond milk, oil and salt. Blend until smooth.

Pour the mixture into the prepared tin. Bake for 30–40 minutes, or until the top is cracked and crusty but the centre is still nice and fudgy.

Remove the brownie from the oven and allow to cool in the tin for 20 minutes, then turn out onto a wire rack to cool for a further 20 minutes.

When cool, cut the brownie into squares, drizzle over the chocolate sauce and top with the raspberries and rose petals. Enjoy immediately, or store in an airtight container in the fridge for up to 1 week.

MAKES 12. GF

MINI VANILLA CUPCAKES
WITH
STRAWBERRY-COCONUT ICING

These little cupcakes are the perfect party treat. No packet mixes, no eggs and no artificial colours. To separate your coconut cream, place the can in the fridge overnight and don't shake it before opening. Scoop out the thick layer at the top – this is the part you want for the icing – and reserve the watery coconut 'milk' for the cake batter.

ICING
1 cup cashews, pre-soaked (see page 18)
⅓ cup chilled coconut cream solids (see recipe introduction)
1 tablespoon coconut oil
100 g strawberries (about 6), plus ½ cup halved fresh or dehydrated strawberries, to decorate
edible flowers, to decorate

CUPCAKES
1 cup (160 g) wholemeal self-raising flour
1 teaspoon baking powder
1½ teaspoons vanilla powder
pinch of salt
2 tablespoons extra-virgin olive oil
2 tablespoons maple syrup
1 cup coconut 'milk' (see recipe introduction)
1 teaspoon chia seeds

To make the icing, place the cashews, coconut cream solids, coconut oil and strawberries in a blender and blend for 3–5 minutes, or until smooth. Transfer to an airtight container and refrigerate for 4–6 hours.

Preheat the oven to 170°C fan-forced (190°C conventional).

To make the cupcakes, sift the flour, baking powder, vanilla and salt into a mixing bowl. In a separate bowl, stir together the oil, maple syrup, coconut 'milk' and chia seeds and allow to sit for 5 minutes.

Pour the wet ingredients into the dry ingredients and stir until just combined.

Spoon the cupcake mixture evenly into a 12-mould silicone mini cupcake tray or a mini muffin tray lined with 12 paper cases. Bake for 25–30 minutes, or until a skewer inserted in the centre of a cupcake comes out clean.

Remove the cupcakes from the oven and leave to cool on the bench for 20 minutes before turning out onto a wire rack to cool for another 30 minutes.

Scoop the set icing mixture into a piping bag fitted with a wide piping nozzle. Pipe the icing over each cupcake. Top each with a fresh strawberry half or dehydrated strawberry and some edible flower petals.

MAKES 10–12

COCONUT PANNA COTTA

This is a really light, easy, low-sugar dessert. It's wobbly, coconutty and VEGAN! Yep, no gelatine here – just agar-agar. Agar-agar powder is made from algae and is often used in Asian desserts. It doesn't have any flavour, so don't worry – your panna cotta will taste amazing.

1 x 400 ml can full-fat coconut milk
¼ cup maple syrup
½ teaspoon vanilla powder
1 teaspoon agar-agar
1 teaspoon tapioca starch (arrowroot)

TO SERVE
finely grated lemon zest
fresh berries
unsalted pistachios, roughly chopped
maple syrup
edible flowers (optional)

Place the coconut milk, maple syrup and vanilla in a small saucepan over a medium heat. Sprinkle in the agar-agar and tapioca, whisking continuously until the mixture begins to boil. Reduce the heat to low and simmer for 3 minutes, whisking continuously, until the mixture thickens.

Pour the mixture evenly into 6–8 silicone cupcake moulds and place in the fridge to set for 2 hours.

To serve, turn out each panna cotta onto a plate and top with the lemon zest, berries, pistachios, a drizzle of maple syrup and some edible flowers (if using). Best enjoyed immediately!

SERVES 6–8, GF

NEAPOLITAN NICE-CREAM SUNDAE

Nice-cream is a really healthy, super-quick vegan ice cream. No waiting around for an ice-cream maker to churn away. All you need are some frozen bananas and a good-quality blender. This is so healthy you can have it for breakfast or as a light summer dessert. If you're making this for one person, use two bananas and halve the rest of the ingredients. You also have to move quickly, otherwise it will begin to melt.

6 peeled frozen bananas
2 tablespoons coconut yoghurt or Almond Milk
   (see recipe page 279)
½ teaspoon vanilla powder
½ cup frozen strawberries
2 tablespoons cacao powder
2 tablespoons roughly chopped vegan dark chocolate

Place the bananas, coconut yoghurt or almond milk and the vanilla powder in a blender and blitz until smooth and creamy.

Scoop two-thirds of the banana/vanilla mixture into a bowl and pop it in the freezer.

Add the strawberries to the remaining mixture in the blender and blend until smooth. Transfer to another bowl and place in the freezer.

Remove the banana/vanilla mixture from the freezer and return half of that mixture to the blender. Add the cacao powder and blitz for 5 seconds.

Divide the chocolate nice-cream among two or three serving bowls and quickly add the banana/vanilla and strawberry nice-creams from the freezer. Scatter the chocolate over the top and dive in immediately!

SERVES 2–3, GF

MY NANNA'S RICE PUDDING

Okay, this recipe is obviously one I hold dear to my heart. We used to visit my nan every holidays, and I remember sitting with her while she made rice pudding. I loved watching it bubble away in the oven and form a golden, milky skin on top. This is a classic English dessert, and I think it's the smell of the nutmeg wafting through the house that I remember the most. My dairy-free version is not quite the same as Nan's, but it sure is delicious. Serve this warm.

1 cup white rice
750 ml soy milk (or 1 x 400 ml can full-fat coconut milk
    and 1½ cups water), plus extra if required
75 g medjool dates (about 4), pitted
1 teaspoon ground nutmeg
½ teaspoon ground cinnamon
½ teaspoon vanilla powder
pinch of salt

TO SERVE
fresh seasonal fruit
edible flowers (optional)
1 tablespoon roughly chopped almonds, pre-soaked
    (see page 18)
soy or coconut milk (optional)

Preheat the oven to 170°C fan-forced (190°C conventional).

Place the rice in a 20 cm square baking dish.

Place the milk, dates, spices, vanilla and salt in a blender and blend until smooth. Pour the mixture over the rice and stir well. Bake for 30–45 minutes, or until the rice is cooked through and the top is golden. Check after 25 minutes and if the rice has soaked up all of the milk, add another ½ cup.

Serve the pudding hot, topped with the fresh fruit, edible flowers (if using), chopped almonds and an extra splash of milk, if desired.

SERVES 4–6. GF

MISO-CARAMEL MACADAMIA CUPS

The gooey salted caramel centre in these little gems is *totally* droolworthy. Medjool dates are full of fibre and create that perfect thick, smooth texture, plus they naturally have a caramelised sweetness. Don't get me wrong, though – they are really rich, so you will only need one little maca cup to satisfy your caramel cravings. I've added the miso for saltiness. Once you've tried one of these, you will want to show the world just what you can create with plant-based wholefoods. Store them in the freezer: the caramel won't freeze but this keeps the base nice and firm.

BASE
1½ cups (230 g) macadamia nuts, pre-soaked (see page 18)
75 g medjool dates (about 4), pitted
½ cup desiccated coconut

MISO-CARAMEL FILLING
320 g medjool dates (about 18), pitted
1 tablespoon miso paste
⅓ cup maple syrup
1 tablespoon macadamia oil

TOPPING
50 g coconut oil
50 g cacao butter
½ cup cacao powder
¼ cup maple syrup

TO SERVE
6 rosemary sprigs, quartered
roughly chopped macadamia nuts
salt

To make the base, place the macadamias in a blender and process until finely crumbled. Add the dates and process again until you have a rough, dough-like mixture. Transfer to a mixing bowl and stir in the coconut. Mix well. Press the mixture into the base and sides of a 24 mould silicone cupcake tray (or use a regular muffin tray lined with baking paper). Place in the freezer to set.

To make the filling, combine all the ingredients in a blender and blitz until smooth and creamy.

When the base has set, remove from the freezer and spoon 1 dessertspoon of filling evenly into each mould. Return to the freezer.

To make the topping, melt the coconut oil and cacao butter in a heatproof bowl over a saucepan of simmering water. Remove the pan from the heat and sift in the cacao powder. Add the maple syrup and whisk with a fork until well combined.

When the caramel is cold, pour the chocolate over each mould. Return to the freezer to set for at least 1 hour.

To serve, remove the 'cups' from their moulds and top with the rosemary sprigs, a sprinkle of macadamias and a twist of salt.

MAKES 24. GF

WARM STICKY DATE PUDDING

Who doesn't love a good sticky date, right? I promise you – this is one of the most delicious treats you will ever bake. Just the aroma while it's cooking is mouth-watering. Plus, it's high in fibre from the wholemeal spelt flour, chia seeds and dates. Spelt flour is made from a species of wheat that contains less gluten, which means some people find it easier to digest. It also means you need to be gentle when stirring the mixture because over-mixing can destroy the properties of the gluten that help the dough to rise.

1 cup (150 g) wholemeal spelt flour
1 teaspoon bicarbonate of soda
1 teaspoon baking powder
1 teaspoon vanilla powder
¼ teaspoon salt
1 cup soy milk or other non-dairy milk (see recipes page 279)
2 teaspoons chia seeds
2 tablespoons maple syrup
110 g medjool dates (about 6), pitted
¼ cup extra-virgin olive oil

STICKY DATE SAUCE
250 g medjool dates (about 14), pitted
½ cup soy milk
¼ teaspoon salt
¼ teaspoon vanilla powder

Preheat the oven to 170°C fan-forced (190°C conventional). Line a 15 cm x 10 cm loaf tin with baking paper.

Sift the flour, bicarbonate of soda, baking powder, vanilla and salt into a mixing bowl. Make a well in the centre and set aside.

Place the milk, chia seeds, maple syrup, dates and oil in a food processor or blender and blend for 45 seconds, or until smooth. Pour into the dry ingredients and stir gently until just combined. Transfer to the prepared tin and bake for 25 minutes.

Meanwhile, to make the sticky date sauce, place all the ingredients in a blender with 1 cup of water and blend until smooth.

Remove the pudding from the oven and allow to rest for 5 minutes. Pour over the sticky date sauce and return the pudding to the oven for a further 20 minutes.

Allow the pudding to rest for 5 minutes before serving warm as is, or with a scoop of vegan ice cream or coconut yoghurt.

SERVES 4–6

Isn't this cake beautiful? Just looking at it makes me want to bake it again. Carrot cake is my all-time favourite. I love the mix of spices, the texture of the walnuts and the gooey sweetness of the dates and carrots — *so* scrumptious! And then there's the goodness. You've got antioxidants in the carrot and lemon, long-lasting energy in the flour, and walnuts are believed to be neuro-protective due to their vitamin E, melatonin, folate and omega-3 fatty acid content — they even look like little brains.

1 cup (150 g) self-raising flour
1 cup (150 g) wholemeal spelt flour
2 teaspoons baking powder
1 teaspoon bicarbonate of soda
1 teaspoon ground nutmeg
1 tablespoon ground cinnamon
1 teaspoon vanilla powder
½ teaspoon salt
190 g carrot (about 2), grated
zest and juice of 1 lemon
¼ cup roughly chopped walnuts, pre-soaked (see page 18),
   plus 1 tablespoon extra to serve
180 g medjool dates (about 10), pitted, 3 roughly chopped
1½ cups Almond Milk (see recipe page 279)
⅓ cup extra-virgin olive oil
1 tablespoon flaxseeds
500 g coconut yoghurt
2 cups mixed fresh berries or other seasonal fruit
edible flowers, to decorate
lemon slices, to decorate
1 teaspoon poppy seeds, to decorate (optional)

Preheat the oven to 180°C fan-forced (200°C conventional). Grease a 20 cm round cake tin or line it with baking paper.

Sift the flours, baking powder, bicarbonate of soda, spices, vanilla and salt into a large mixing bowl. Add the carrot, lemon zest, walnuts and the three chopped medjool dates and toss until well combined.

Place the lemon juice, almond milk, oil, flaxseeds and remaining dates in a food processor or blender and blitz until smooth.

Make a well in the centre of the dry ingredients. Pour in the wet mixture and stir until just combined (don't over-mix). Transfer to the prepared tin and bake for 40–50 minutes, or until a skewer inserted in the centre of the cake comes out clean.

Remove the cake from the oven and allow to cool in the tin for 20 minutes. Turn out onto a wire rack and leave to cool for a further 20–30 minutes.

When completely cool, cut the cake horizontally into two even layers. Place the bottom layer on a cake stand or serving plate. Spread it with half of the yoghurt and evenly sprinkle over half of the berries and walnuts. Top with the remaining cake layer, yoghurt, berries and walnuts, then finish with the flowers and lemon slices and a sprinkle of poppy seeds, if desired.

TIP
This is delicious served fresh, but you can also store it in a covered container in the fridge for up to 5 days.

LEMON COCO-BERRY TART

This coconut and lemon dessert is perfect for summer picnics or dinner parties. The fresh berries on top add a burst of colour and flavour. Berries are naturally lower in fructose than other fruits, which is great if you know you have fructose malabsorption. They're also high in antioxidants. Fresh raspberries are my favourite. I've used dried figs instead of dates in the base to give a different flavour. Figs are really high in fibre but also have a perfectly sticky texture to hold the base together.

1 cup almonds, pre-soaked (see page 18)
1 cup coconut flakes
60 g dried figs
1 cup cashews, pre-soaked (see page 18)
1 cup coconut yoghurt
zest and juice of 1 lemon
1 tablespoon coconut oil
1 cup fresh berries
lemon slices, to serve
edible flowers, to serve (optional)

TIPS

- *You may like to add 4–5 drops of lemon essential oil (food grade) to enhance the lemon flavour.*
- *To keep this for longer, place it in a sealed container in the freezer (minus the berries) for up to 2 weeks. To serve, allow to thaw for 15–20 minutes, then top with the berries.*

To make the base, place the almonds and coconut flakes in a food processor or blender and blitz to a rough crumble. Add the figs and 2 tablespoons of water and process until the figs are broken down and the mixture is starting to clump together. Press the mixture into the base and side of a 20 cm loose-bottomed tart tin.

To make the filling, place the cashews, coconut yoghurt and lemon zest and juice in a food processor or blender and blitz until smooth. Add the coconut oil and process for another 30 seconds. Spread the mixture over the base and smooth out flat. Top with the berries, lemon slices and edible flowers (if using) and place in the fridge, covered, for 2–4 hours to set. Slice and serve immediately.

SERVES 8–12. GF

BLACK SESAME AND
GREEN TEA RAW CAKE

This awesome tower cake looks like something out of a fairytale and is perfect for a special occasion. In fact, I made it for my twin sister's birthday one year – which means I kind of made it for me, too! The combination of black sesame and green tea is inspired by Japanese desserts, and they taste so yummy together. You can also add a pinch of spirulina powder to bring out the green colour. I've used star-shaped silicone ice-cube trays to create the magical stars on top of this cake. Once it all comes together it looks *so* amazing.

BASE
1 cup almonds, pre-soaked (see page 18)
½ cup desiccated coconut
90 g medjool dates (about 5), pitted
¼ cup cacao powder
2 tablespoons tahini

FILLINGS
3 cups cashews, pre-soaked (see page 18)
¼ cup maple syrup
1 x 400 ml can full-fat coconut cream
⅓ cup coconut oil
⅓ cup black sesame seeds
¼ cup cacao powder
½ avocado
zest and juice of 1 lime
1 teaspoon matcha powder

TOPPING
1 cup Raw Chocolate Sauce (see recipe page 295)
¼ teaspoon matcha powder
¼ teaspoon cacao powder

Line the base of two 11 cm springform cake tins with baking paper.

To make the base layer, place the almonds and coconut in a food processor or blender and blitz to a fine crumb. Add the dates and cacao powder and blend until the mixture forms a moist crumble. Transfer to a mixing bowl with the tahini and knead with your hands until well combined. Press the mixture into the base of one of the prepared tins and place in the freezer while you make the filling.

To make the filling, place the cashews in a blender with the maple syrup and coconut cream. Blend for 4–5 minutes, or until smooth. Add the coconut oil and blend on high for another 30 seconds. Pour half the filling mixture into a bowl and set aside.

To make the chocolate layer, add the black sesame seeds and cacao powder to the mixture in the blender and blend on high for 60 seconds. Pour three-quarters of the chocolate mixture over the cake base and return to the freezer for 4–6 hours. Spoon the remaining chocolate mixture into a star-shaped silicone ice-cube tray and place in the freezer to set for 4–6 hours.

To make the green tea layer, first wash out the blender. Transfer the remaining filling mixture to the blender along with the avocado, lime zest and juice and matcha.

▶

Blend on high for 60 seconds. Pour three-quarters of the green tea mixture into the other prepared tin. Reserve 2 tablespoons of the mixture for decorating (keep it in the fridge). Spoon the remaining mixture into a star-shaped silicone ice-cube tray and place in the freezer, along with the base, chocolate and green tea layers, for 4–6 hours.

When you're ready to assemble the cake, make up a batch of raw chocolate sauce. Remove the base and chocolate layers from the tin and carefully transfer to a plate or cake stand. Remove all of the cake layers from the freezer. Using a spatula, spread

the 2 tablespoons of the reserved green tea mixture over the chocolate layer. Remove the green tea layer from the tin and place on top of the chocolate layer. Pop the star shapes out of their silicone trays. Drizzle over the raw chocolate sauce and arrange the stars on the cake. Sprinkle with matcha and cacao powder.

Store the finished cake in the freezer and remove 10–15 minutes before serving, to soften a little. Slice and serve immediately.

SERVES 12, GF

TIP

Don't worry if you only have one springform tin; you can still achieve the same result, but you'll need to start the recipe a day in advance. Instead of pouring the green tea mixture into a second tin, place it in a bowl in the fridge till the other layers are frozen. When ready, transfer the base and chocolate layers to a plate and return to the freezer. Line the tin with fresh baking paper and continue making the green tea layer.

ESPRESSO GANACHE TART

Coffee and chocolate have got to be two of the best things in the world, right? This completely decadent dessert has everything: the smooth, rich flavours of almonds, dates and chocolate and the earthy bitterness of coffee beans. If you're having this before bed it may leave you buzzing!

BASE
1 cup (150 g) almonds, pre-soaked (see page 18)
1 cup (180 g) buckwheat, pre-soaked (see page 18)
110 g medjool dates (about 6), pitted
¼ cup cacao powder
2 tablespoons coconut oil

FILLING
180 g medjool dates (about 10), pitted
3 espresso shots
⅓ teaspoon salt
¼ cup maple syrup
¼ cup coconut oil
½ cup cacao powder

TOPPING
1 tablespoon coffee beans
30 g vegan dark chocolate, melted
½ teaspoon cacao powder

TIP
*You can store this tart in an
airtight container in the freezer
for up to 4 weeks.*

To make the base, place the almonds and buckwheat in a food processor or blender and blitz to a fine crumb. Add the dates and cacao powder and process until the mixture is moist and holds together. Transfer to a bowl with the coconut oil and mix well with your hands. Press the mixture firmly into the base and side of a 20 cm loose-bottomed tart tin. Place in the freezer while you make the filling.

To make the filling, place the dates, espresso shots, salt and maple syrup in a food processor or blender with ½ cup of water and blitz to a smooth paste. Add the coconut oil and cacao powder and blend until just combined. Be careful not to over-process the coconut oil or it will separate from the mixture.

Remove the base from the freezer and spread the filling over evenly. Top the tart with the coffee beans, a drizzle of melted chocolate and a dusting of cacao powder. Place the tart in the freezer to set for 2 hours before slicing and serving.

SERVES 8–12. GF

DRINK
YOUR
WAY TO
BLISSFUL
HEALTH

MOROCCAN SPICED ORANGE JUICE

My sister, Lauren, travels the world, and I often ask her to share her favourite local dishes. This recipe was inspired by her recent trip to Morocco, where she was served fresh orange juice with cinnamon. What I love about orange juice is that you don't need a fancy juicer to make it. Just a simple citrus press or a manual juicer will do the trick.

5 oranges, plus extra slices to serve
1 lemon, plus extra slices to serve
½ teaspoon ground cinnamon
1 cup ice cubes
cinnamon sticks, to serve (optional)

Remove the rind from the oranges and lemon. Cut the flesh into small pieces and feed through the juicer. (If you are using a citrus press, halve the fruit and press or squeeze out the juice.)

Pour the juice into a large jug or jar with a lid. Add the ground cinnamon and ice cubes, seal and shake.

Serve immediately with extra slices of orange and lemon and a cinnamon stick, if desired.

SERVES 2-3

GREEN JUICE

BEET BLISS

This green juice recipe is my favourite – it's so refreshing. I love to throw in a heap of extra ice cubes and take it to the beach.

1 cucumber, trimmed
1 lemon, rind removed
2 cups chopped lettuce leaves
large handful of baby spinach leaves
2 apples
small handful of mint leaves, reserve 2 sprigs to serve
handful of ice cubes

Cut all of the fruits and vegetables into chunks and feed them through your juicer along with the mint. Pour the juice into two jars or glasses. Add the ice cubes and serve with a sprig of mint.

SERVES 2

I love the earthy flavour of beetroot, especially combined with carrot. If you're new to beet juice, this is a great way to try it. The coconut water and strawberries give it a lighter, subtly sweet taste. Plus, the bright red colour is just gorgeous.

1 beetroot
2 large carrots
1 lemon, rind removed
10 strawberries, hulled
1 cup coconut water
handful of ice cubes

Cut all of the fruits and vegetables into small chunks and feed them through your juicer. Pour into two jars or glasses with the coconut water and a handful of ice cubes.

SERVES 2

STRAWBERRY LEMONADE

If you don't like drinking plain soda water, try this delicious mocktail. Most strawberry lemonades contain around 6 teaspoons of sugar per 250 ml, which is outrageous! This recipe contains less than 1 teaspoon per cup. The lemon and strawberry give it a subtle sweetness that's also refreshing – perfect for summer afternoon picnics.

juice of 2 lemons
200 g strawberries, hulled
750 ml soda water
1 cup ice cubes
1 tablespoon edible flowers and/or dehydrated rose petals

Place the lemon juice and strawberries in a blender and process on high for 1 minute. Strain the mixture through a fine sieve into a large serving jug. Add the soda water, ice cubes and edible flowers and/or rose petals. Serve immediately in cold, tall glasses.

SERVES 4

TIP

Dehydrated rose petals are available from Asian supermarkets and health-food stores. Try the tea section. If you can't find any, use lavender or mint sprigs instead.

CHOC THICKSHAKE

This is the perfect smoothie for when you're feeling like something a little bit cheeky! The trick is to let your bananas ripen until the skins get a bit spotty – this makes them sweeter, as the starches turn to sugars – and then peel and freeze them. Look out for discounted overripe bananas at fresh food markets.

1 large, peeled frozen banana
1 cup Cashew Milk or other non-dairy milk
   (see recipes page 279)
2 medjool dates, pitted
2 tablespoons coconut yoghurt
1 heaped teaspoon cacao powder
1 teaspoon chopped nuts (almond, macadamia),
   pre-soaked (see page 18)
2 ice cubes

TO SERVE
1 tablespoon coconut yoghurt
1 teaspoon cacao nibs
1 tablespoon shredded coconut
1 teaspoon maple syrup
1 teaspoon chopped macadamia nuts,
   pre-soaked (see page 18)
2 teaspoons roughly chopped dark chocolate

Place the banana, milk, dates, coconut yoghurt, cacao, nuts and ice in a blender and blend until smooth. Pour into a tall glass or jar and top with the coconut yoghurt, cacao nibs, shredded coconut, maple syrup, macadamias and dark chocolate. Enjoy with a spoon and a straw.

SERVES 1

GOLDEN BLISS SMOOTHIE

Turmeric is an Indian spice well known for its health benefits. Its main component, curcumin, has anti-inflammatory properties, and researchers are investigating its effects on arthritis and neurodegenerative diseases such as Alzheimer's. I love sneaking some extra turmeric into my diet wherever I can. Turmeric lattes are a delicious warming drink to enjoy in winter, but this smoothie will give you a turmeric fix all summer long.

2 peeled frozen bananas
1 cup Almond Milk or other non-dairy milk (see recipes
    page 279)
½ teaspoon ground turmeric, plus extra to serve (optional)
¼ teaspoon ground ginger
pinch of freshly ground black pepper
1 medjool date, pitted
4 ice cubes

Place all the ingredients in a blender and blitz until smooth. Pour into a jar and top with a sprinkle of turmeric, if desired. Enjoy immediately.

SERVES 1 (OR 2 SMALLER SERVES)

TIP

If you are new to turmeric and still unsure about the flavour, try halving the amount in this recipe and gradually building up to more.

The best
preventative
medicine
is a
healthy diet

PEANUT BUTTER JELLY TIME

Fruit and nuts are a winning combo, especially berries and peanuts. Frozen bananas are an excellent base for any smoothie, as they give it a nice thick and creamy consistency. I also love bananas because they're high in vitamin C, potassium and manganese.

½ cup frozen raspberries
2 peeled frozen bananas
2 tablespoons natural peanut butter (see Tip page 286)
¾ cup Almond Milk or other non-dairy milk (see recipes page 279)
½ cup ice cubes

TIP
If you don't have any raspberries to hand, you can also make this with strawberries or blueberries, or even some of my Berry Nice Jam (page 292).

Place the raspberries in a bowl with 1 tablespoon of warm water and set aside to thaw.

Place the bananas, 1 tablespoon of the peanut butter, the milk and ice cubes in a blender and blend until smooth.

Mash the raspberries with a fork and pour into the base of two glasses or jars. Pour over the smoothie mixture and top with the remaining peanut butter. Slurp it up!

SERVES 2

PURPLE DREAM

This beautifully coloured smoothie is brilliant for those mornings when you need a quick breakfast on the go. I've used frozen papaya for the base but banana or mango also work perfectly. Maqui berry powder is a freeze-dried powder from South America, which (like açai berry powder) adds an extra dose of antioxidants to your morning smoothie and brightens the deep purple colour. If you can't find either of these ingredients in your local health-food store, just throw in an extra handful of blueberries instead.

1 cup frozen chopped papaya or mango (or 1 large, peeled frozen banana)
½ cup frozen blueberries
1 cup Coconut Rice Milk or other non-dairy milk (see recipes page 279)
2 tablespoons rolled oats
1 teaspoon chia seeds
1 teaspoon maqui berry or açai powder (optional)
1 tablespoon rice and pea protein powder (optional)

Place all the ingredients in a blender and blend on high speed for 30–60 seconds. Pour into a tall glass or jar and enjoy.

SERVES 1 (OR 2 SMALLER SERVES)

TIP
You can refrigerate this for up to 4 hours before drinking.

DREAMY DRAGON SMOOTHIE

In Bali over Christmas, I had dragon fruit (pitaya) pretty much every day. Its deep pink colour and lovely texture is perfect for smoothies, and I simply had to share the pure bliss of this recipe with you. Dragon fruit is also grown here in Australia in the summer months. I recommend buying a heap when it's in season and freezing them for smoothies.

2 peeled frozen bananas
1 frozen dragon fruit
2 handfuls of ice cubes
1 cup baby spinach leaves (about 50 g)
½ teaspoon spirulina powder (see Tip page 262)
1 tablespoon cashews or almonds, pre-soaked (see page 18)
1 tablespoon natural peanut butter (see Tip page 286)
1 tablespoon cacao powder
½ cup coconut water
½ cup soy milk or Almond Milk (see recipe page 279)
3 tablespoons shredded coconut
1 tablespoon cacao nibs

Place the bananas, dragon fruit, ice cubes, spinach, spirulina, nuts, peanut butter, cacao powder, coconut water, soy or almond milk and 2 tablespoons of the shredded coconut in a blender and blitz on high until smooth and creamy. The texture should be thick enough to hold a spoon upright, but runny enough to get through a wide straw.

Pour the smoothie into two or three jars or tumblers, and top each with the cacao nibs and the remaining coconut. Dig in with a long spoon and a wide straw.

SERVES 2–3

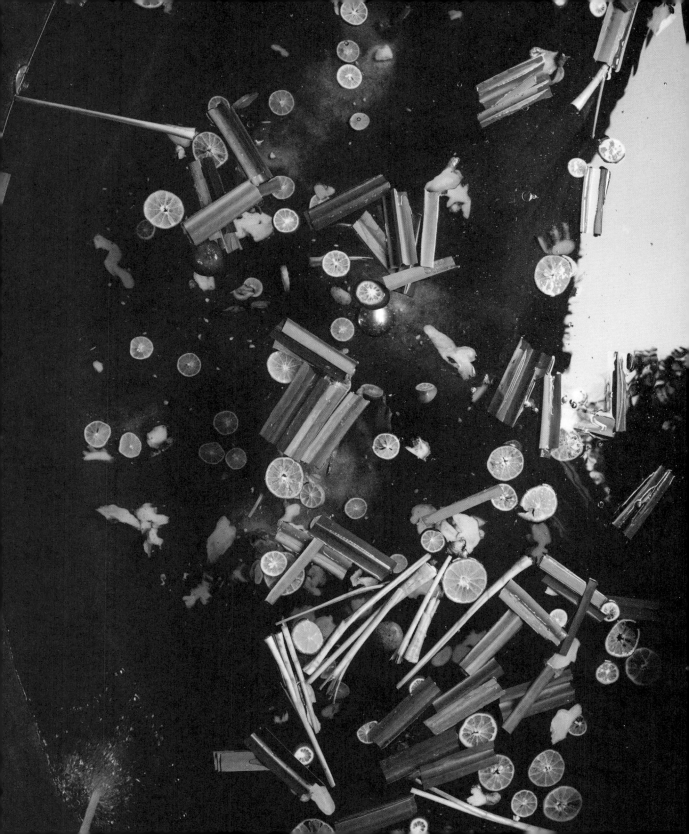

GREEN GODDESS SMOOTHIE

Even if you're not a big fan of green smoothies, you've got to try this baby. It's an excellent way to pack in more serves of vegetables and is just delicious.

2 peeled frozen bananas
½ cup chopped frozen mango
1 cup baby spinach leaves (about 50 g)
1 kale leaf
1 teaspoon chia seeds
1 cup Almond Milk (see recipe page 279) or coconut water
handful of ice cubes
½ teaspoon spirulina powder (optional)

Place all the ingredients in a blender and blitz on high speed for 30–60 seconds, or until smooth. Pour into two jars or glasses. Drink one now and store the other in the fridge for up to 4 hours.

SERVES 2

TIP

Spirulina is an algae that is rich in protein, iron and potassium. It is found in a dry powder form at bulk wholefood and health-food stores.

CHAI TEA SPICE MIX

Chai tea is absolutely delicious. I love making up a batch of this spice mix to get me through the winter. This is also a really nice idea for gifting: make up a double or triple batch, pop it in pretty jars and attach handmade gift tags.

4 cinnamon sticks
1 teaspoon fennel seeds
1 teaspoon ground ginger
1 teaspoon vanilla powder
8 cloves
10 cardamom pods
2 star anise
1 tablespoon black tea leaves

Place all the ingredients in a jar. Seal and shake vigorously. Store in a cool, dry place for up to 6 months.

SERVES 6–8

CHAI LATTE

Chai lattes served in cafes are often made from powders and syrups that contain loads of added sugars and artificial flavours. This is a much more traditional way to have chai, and the flavours of the different spices are *so* much richer.

1 heaped teaspoon of Chai Tea Spice Mix (see recipe page 264)
1 cup soy milk or homemade nut milk (see recipes page 279)
ground cinnamon, to serve
edible flowers, to serve (optional)
maple syrup, to serve (optional)

Place the spice mix and 1 cup of water in a small saucepan over a medium–high heat. Bring to the boil, reduce the heat and simmer for 5 minutes. Add the milk and stir.

Once the mixture is hot (just before boiling), remove the pan from the heat and pour through a strainer over a mug. Sprinkle with the cinnamon and edible flowers (if using) and stir in a drizzle of maple syrup, if desired.

SERVES 1–2

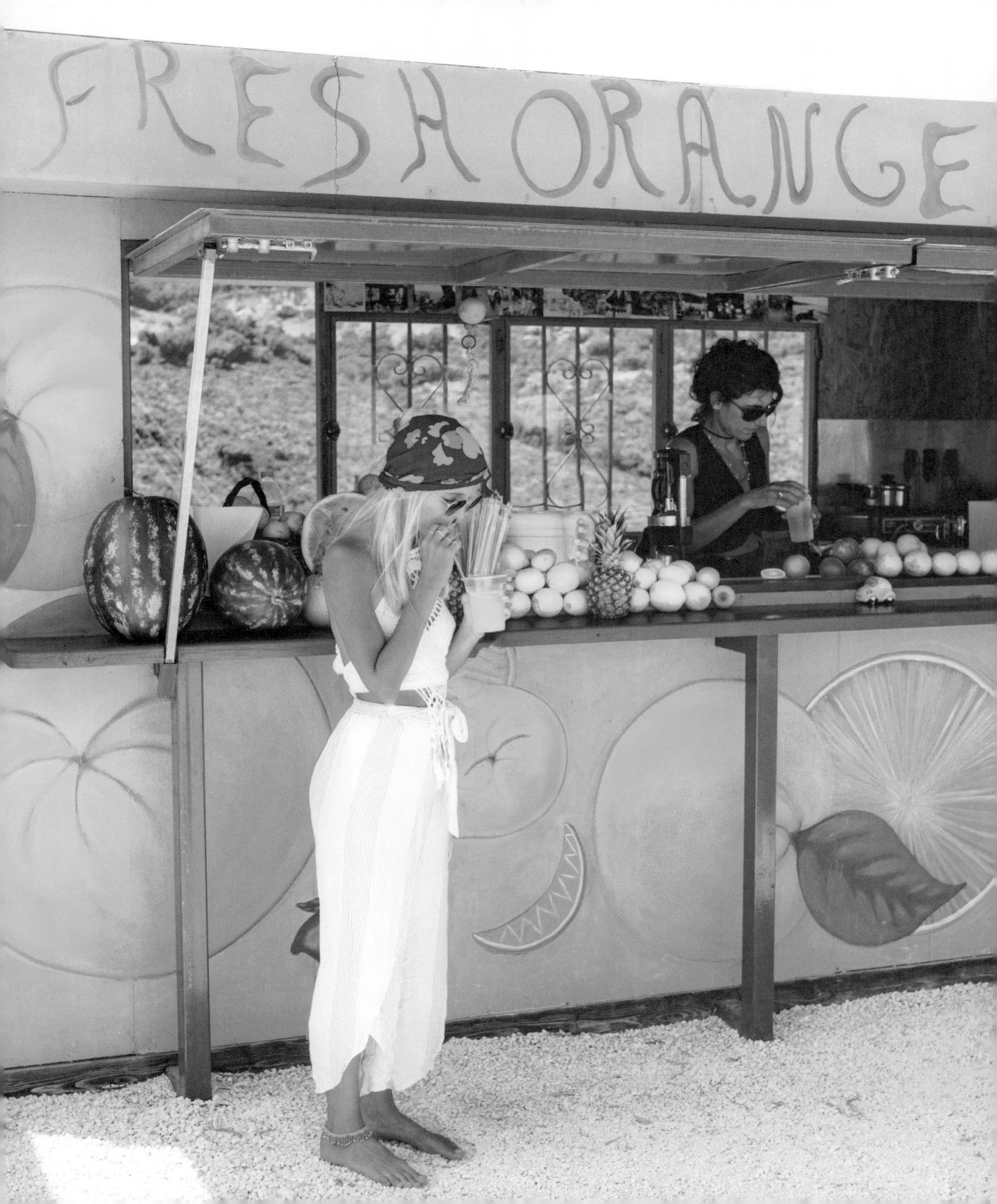
FRESH ORANGE

CHOCOLATE MATCHA LATTE

Matcha is a traditional Japanese tea made from ground green tea leaves. Green tea is high in antioxidants and also contains the amino acid L-theanine, which can make you feel more relaxed. To mix things up, I have added some cacao powder for a light chocolate taste, though feel free to leave this out if you prefer a simple matcha drink.

1 cup Coconut Rice Milk or other non-dairy milk
  (see recipes page 279)
1 teaspoon matcha powder
½ teaspoon cacao powder
½ teaspoon maple syrup

Place the milk in a saucepan over a medium heat until hot but not boiling. Remove from the heat. Add the matcha powder, cacao powder and maple syrup and whisk vigorously using a matcha bamboo whisk (or transfer to a blender and blend on medium speed). Serve immediately in your favourite mug.

SERVES 1

SPICY HOT CHOCOLATE

This healthy hot chocolate is the perfect winter afternoon treat. Cacao powder is made from cold-pressed cocoa beans, which means more of the nutrients remain intact compared to cocoa powder (which undergoes processing at high temperatures). It's best to use cacao powder for maximum antioxidant, vitamin and mineral content, however, you can use cocoa powder if you prefer (just don't confuse it with the sweetened drinking chocolate!). The addition of cayenne pepper and ginger gives this a spicy punch.

300 ml Almond Milk or other non-dairy milk (see recipes page 279)
1 heaped teaspoon cacao powder
tiny pinch of ground cayenne pepper, or to taste
pinch of ground ginger
1 teaspoon maple syrup

Heat the milk in a saucepan over a medium heat until hot but not boiling. Take off the heat, add the remaining ingredients and whisk vigorously. Pour into a mug and enjoy.

SERVES 1

A HEALTHY KITCHEN IS ALL ABOUT GOOD BASICS

NON-DAIRY MILKS

We make all of our non-dairy milks at home, and they taste sooo much better than store-bought versions, which often contain added sugar, salt and vegetable oil. People expect it to be time-consuming to make your own milk, but it actually doesn't take too long once you get the hang of it and start incorporating it into your weekly routine. Note that these milks contain no additives, so they usually only last up to a week in the fridge. It's important to allow nuts, seeds and grains to soak for at least 8 hours (or overnight), as it reduces the phytate content and allows micronutrients such as calcium, zinc and iron to be better absorbed.

ALMOND MILK

1 cup almonds, pre-soaked (see page 18)
½ teaspoon vanilla powder

Drain the almonds and rinse well in fresh water. Place in a blender with the vanilla and 1 litre of water. Blend on high for 2–3 minutes until white and frothy.

Place a piece of cheesecloth or muslin over a jug or bowl with a lip. Pour in the almond puree. Gather the edges of the cloth together and wring out all of the liquid. (You can also use a nut-milk bag if you have one.) Transfer the liquid to a clean jar or bottle, seal and refrigerate for up to 1 week.

MAKES 1 LITRE

CASHEW MILK

1 cup cashews, pre-soaked (see page 18)
¼ teaspoon ground cinnamon

Drain and rinse the cashews and place in a blender with 1 litre of water and the cinnamon. Continue method as per the Almond Milk recipe.

MAKES 1 LITRE

COCONUT RICE MILK

½ cup coconut flakes
½ cup brown rice

Place the coconut flakes and rice in a bowl, cover with water and set aside to soak for at least 8 hours, or overnight. Or, if you like, you can use leftover cooked rice and soaked coconut flakes.

The next day, drain and rinse the coconut and rice and place in a blender with 1 litre of water. Continue method as per the Almond Milk recipe.

MAKES 1 LITRE

TIP
Try fortifying your milks with 1–3 calcium and vitamin D tablets to ensure healthy bones.

HERBY ALMOND FETA

I love to serve this on a big platter with some crackers, dried fruit and dip to share with friends. Leftovers can be sliced up and thrown in a salad or crumbled on sourdough with smashed avocado.

1½ cups almonds, pre-soaked (see page 18)
⅓ cup lemon juice
¼ cup extra-virgin olive oil, plus extra for drizzling
1 teaspoon salt
2 teaspoons dried rosemary
2 teaspoons dried thyme

Preheat the oven to 180°C fan-forced (200°C conventional). Lightly oil a baking tray or line it with baking paper.

Drain and rinse the almonds. Place in a food processor or blender with the lemon juice, oil, salt and ¼ cup of water. Blend until smooth, thick and creamy. You may need to add some extra water (up to ½ cup) to get it moving, but it should still stick to a spoon turned upside down. Add half each of the rosemary and thyme and stir through with a spoon.

Scoop the mixture out of the processor or blender and, using your hands, shape into one large round (thick and flat on top like a wheel of cheese), or two smaller rounds. Transfer to the prepared tray. Drizzle with the extra oil and sprinkle over the remaining herbs. Bake for 20 minutes, or until golden all over.

Serve warm or cold. Leftovers can be stored in the fridge in a sealed container for up to 5 days.

MAKES 450 G, GF

CASHEW CREAM CHEESE

Cashew cream cheese is a true vegan staple. I use this tasty version as my 'sour cream' on nachos and tacos, as my 'mayo' on burgers and as a delicious pizza topper. Leftovers are wonderful on salads, baked veggies or as a dip for veggie sticks. Nutritional yeast is the key ingredient to getting that cheesy flavour. Most nutritional yeast flakes are fortified with vitamin B12, an important nutrient that's found only in animal products.

1½ cups cashews, pre-soaked (see page 18)
1 teaspoon garlic flakes
1 tablespoon apple cider vinegar
¼ cup nutritional yeast
¼ teaspoon salt
juice of 1 lemon

TIP
*Add more water, lemon juice
and oil if you want a
runnier consistency.*

Drain the cashews and transfer to a food processor or blender with the rest of the ingredients and ¼ cup of water. Blend until smooth and creamy, adding extra water (in ¼ cup increments) until the mixture reaches the desired consistency. Store in a sealed container in the fridge for up to 5 days.

MAKES 2 CUPS, GF

PEANUT SESAME BUTTER

It's so easy and so much healthier to make your own peanut butter — especially since many store-bought versions are high in salt and contain added sugars. Peanuts are actually a legume (the same family as beans, lentils and chickpeas), so they're high in monounsaturated fats and are a good source of protein and minerals. I love to spread my homemade peanut butter on toast, blend it into a smoothie, or serve it with fresh fruit and veggie sticks.

1½ cups unsalted, dry-roasted peanuts
2 tablespoons sesame seeds
2 tablespoons sesame oil
1 teaspoon vanilla powder
½ teaspoon salt

Place all the ingredients in a food processor or blender and process until smooth and creamy. Transfer to a clean jar, seal and store in the fridge for up to 4 weeks.

MAKES 300 G, GF

TIPS

- *To make natural peanut butter, simply omit the sesame seeds and sesame oil, and use peanut oil instead.*
- *For something deliciously different, try adding 1 teaspoon of ground cinnamon or 2 teaspoons of cacao powder.*

GOOEY CARAMEL PASTE

Medjool dates are like little gooey, golden fruits of bliss! They have a sweet caramel taste, are packed with fibre and have the perfect texture for making fudgy, sweet pastes. My partner, Alex, is caramel obsessed, so I was pretty excited to discover this healthy alternative. We love it on pancakes, blended through smoothies and dolloped on a nice-cream sundae. It makes a great replacement for sugar in any recipe.

360 g medjool dates (about 20), pitted

Place the dates in a food processor or blender with 1 cup of water and blitz until smooth and creamy. The paste should be thick enough to stick to a spoon held upside down. Transfer the paste to a jar, seal and refrigerate for up to 2 weeks.

MAKES 2 CUPS. GF

TIPS

- *To make it last longer, freeze half of the batch in an airtight container (it'll keep for up to 1 month). Just allow it to thaw for 10 minutes before using.*
- *It's best to use medjool dates for this recipe. Other varieties would need to be soaked in warm water first.*

BERRY NICE JAM

Now that you have a peanut butter recipe (see page 286) it would be silly not to enjoy it with some homemade jam! Store-bought jams are not only loaded with sugar (often more than 60 per cent!) but also have very little nutritional value, as the fruit has been heated to very high temperatures, destroying vitamin C and other nutrients. This jam recipe is super easy, though it only lasts about a week in the fridge, so you may want to freeze any leftovers if you don't plan to use it all in the coming days. I love this on toast, on smoothie bowls and in my jam drops (see recipe page 182).

150 g fresh or frozen raspberries
1 tablespoon lemon juice
2 tablespoons chia seeds
1 tablespoon warm water

TIP
This is delicious with any fresh or frozen berry. Try strawberries, blueberries, blackberries, loganberries or whatever berries you can source.

If using frozen raspberries, allow them to thaw on the bench for 20 minutes first.

Place all the ingredients in a food processor or blender and pulse until just combined. Or, if you prefer your jam a bit chunky, place in a bowl and mash with a fork. Transfer to a jar, seal and refrigerate for up to 1 week.

MAKES 1 CUP, GF

RAW CHOCOLATE SAUCE

I incorporate this simple raw chocolate recipe into many of my dessert creations. It uses just four ingredients, which you can tinker with to suit your taste – more cacao if you like a more intense flavour, or more maple syrup if you prefer things sweeter. Use this for dunking fruit in, pouring over cakes and slices or as topping on a sundae. I love to drizzle it over my nice-cream – it makes an instant crunchy chocolate topper (the coconut oil hardens on contact with anything cold).

¼ cup (50 g) cacao butter
¼ cup (50 g) coconut oil
½ cup (50 g) cacao powder
¼ cup (60 ml) maple syrup

TIP
Make a double batch and freeze the extra sauce in ice-cube trays. Transfer the frozen cubes to a sealed container in the freezer, where it will last for up to 1 month. Thaw and melt as needed.

Place the cacao butter and coconut oil in a heatproof bowl over a saucepan of simmering water. Stir with a metal spoon until melted.

Remove the pan from the heat and whisk in the cacao powder and maple syrup. Remove the bowl from the pan and set aside to cool for 5–10 minutes to allow the sauce to thicken.

MAKES 1 CUP

Eat
more
plants!

CREAMY GUACAMOLE

This is one of my favourite dips ever! The cashews not only give it that extra creaminess but also boost the protein content and provide a good source of iron, copper, magnesium and zinc. Paired with some baked sweet potato chips (see page 314), this is your ultimate movie night snack.

½ cup cashews, pre-soaked (see page 18)
¼ cup chopped coriander leaves and stalks,
    plus extra leaves to serve
1 spring onion, roughly chopped
juice of 1 lime
1 large avocado, roughly chopped
pinch of salt
TO SERVE
1 long red chilli, sliced
½ teaspoon smoked paprika
1 tablespoon extra-virgin olive oil
1 teaspoon habañero chilli sauce, or other chilli sauce

Place the cashews, coriander, spring onion and lime juice in a food processor or blender with ½ cup of water and blend until the mixture begins to form a paste. Add the avocado and salt and blend for a further 30 seconds, or until smooth.

Transfer to a serving bowl and top with the chilli, paprika, olive oil, chilli sauce and extra coriander leaves. Store leftovers in a sealed container in the fridge for up to 2 days.

MAKES 1 CUP, GF

TRADITIONAL HUMMUS

Hummus is a Middle Eastern dip made from chickpeas and is a staple ingredient in my home. It not only tastes epic on just about everything but also happens to be super good for you. Chickpeas are a legume and are considered a 'meat alternative', because they not only contain the fibre, carbohydrates and vitamins associated with vegetables but are also good sources of plant proteins, iron and zinc. You can serve this versatile staple as a dip with crackers and veggie sticks, spread on burgers, pizzas or toast, or even dolloped on salads.

1 x 400 g can chickpeas, drained and rinsed
¼ cup extra-virgin olive oil, plus extra to serve (optional)
⅓ cup lemon juice
½ teaspoon salt
2 tablespoons tahini
1 teaspoon ground cumin
1 garlic clove, crushed

TO SERVE
sesame seeds
coriander leaves, finely chopped
chilli flakes (optional)
edible flowers (optional)

Place all the ingredients in a food processor or blender with ¼ cup of water. Blitz to a smooth paste, adding an extra ¼ cup of water if the mixture is too dry.

Transfer the hummus to a serving bowl and, if you like, drizzle with a little more olive oil. Sprinkle over some sesame seeds and coriander, and some chilli flakes and edible flowers, if desired. Store leftovers in a sealed container in the fridge for up to 5 days.

MAKES 1½ CUPS. GF

TIP

For a spicy twist to your hummus, add 1 teaspoon of smoked paprika. If you like it hotter, add 1 heaped teaspoon of finely chopped fresh jalapeño (remove the seeds for a milder spice).

SUPER GREEN PESTO

This recipe was inspired by my trip to Italy last year. I just love how each region has its own specialities. This pesto is based on the Genovese pesto I had in the beautiful seaside villages of Cinque Terre. Traditionally, it contains parmesan, which I've replaced with nutritional yeast. I've also added lemon juice to give my pesto a little more zing. (It helps it last longer, too.)

⅓ cup pine nuts
1 bunch of basil (about 75 g), leaves and stalks roughly chopped, plus extra leaves to serve
juice of 1 lemon
¼ cup extra-virgin olive oil
½ teaspoon salt
2 tablespoons nutritional yeast
2 garlic cloves, roughly chopped
1 cup baby spinach leaves (about 50 g)

Heat a small frying pan over a medium heat. Add the pine nuts and toss in the pan for 1–2 minutes, or until golden. Set aside to cool.

Place the basil, lemon juice, oil, salt, nutritional yeast and garlic in a food processor and blitz until all of the basil is finely chopped. Add the spinach and all but 1 tablespoon of the pine nuts and pulse until the spinach is finely chopped. Transfer to a serving bowl and sprinkle over the remaining pine nuts and a few basil leaves.

Serve as a dip, stirred through freshly cooked pasta or drizzled over pizza. Leftovers can be stored in a sealed jar in the fridge for up to 7 days.

MAKES 1 CUP, GF

FRIJOLE FIESTA DIP

Black beans (also called black turtle beans, or frijole negro in Spanish) make a great meat replacement, as they contain folate, calcium and iron. They are also high in fibre, which not only helps you feel fuller for longer but also keeps you 'regular' (yep, number twos!). Recent research suggests that increasing the amount of beans or legumes in your diet and decreasing your intake of red meat may reduce your risk of bowel cancer. This dip is a delicious filling for tacos, enchiladas and baked sweet potatoes, or simply enjoy it with good old corn chips. It's your ultimate Friday fiesta food.

1 tablespoon extra-virgin olive oil
¼ small red onion, diced, plus extra to serve
1 teaspoon cumin seeds
1 teaspoon ground coriander
1 garlic clove, roughly chopped
1 x 400 g can black beans, drained and rinsed
   (reserve 1 tablespoon to serve)
2 tablespoons sliced, pickled jalapeños, plus extra to serve
pinch of salt
juice of 1 lime

Heat the oil in a frying pan over a medium heat. Add the onion, cumin seeds and coriander and fry for 2 minutes until fragrant. Add the garlic and fry for a further 30 seconds. Transfer the onion mixture to a food processor or blender along with the remaining ingredients and blend until nice and smooth.

Transfer to a bowl and top with the extra onion and black beans and the sliced jalapeño. Serve as a dip or a taco filling. Store leftovers in the fridge in an airtight container for up to 1 week.

MAKES 1½ CUPS, GF

TIP

Pickled jalapeño can be found in the Mexican aisle of the supermarket. Alternatively, you can use a fresh red chilli.

ROASTED GARLIC,
TOMATO AND WHITE BEAN DIP

My absolute favourite way to eat this nutritious dip is dolloped on chunky roasted pumpkin with a side of steamed green vegetables. While roasting the tomatoes reduces the vitamin C content, it actually makes the lycopene (another antioxidant) more bio-available. White beans (cannellini or navy beans) are easy to find in any supermarket.

1 cup halved cherry tomatoes
2 garlic cloves, finely sliced
2 tablespoons extra-virgin olive oil, plus extra
1 tablespoon pine nuts
1 x 400 g can white beans, drained and rinsed
¼ cup almonds, pre-soaked (see page 18)
pinch of salt
1 teaspoon dried mixed herbs
juice of 1 lemon
chilli flakes, to serve (optional)

Preheat the oven to 180°C fan-forced (200°C conventional). Line a baking tray with baking paper.

Place the cherry tomatoes and garlic on the prepared tray and drizzle over the oil. Bake for 20 minutes, or until the tomatoes are soft and the garlic is golden. Sprinkle over the pine nuts and return to the oven for a further 3 minutes. Remove from the oven and set aside to cool for 15 minutes.

Meanwhile, place the white beans, almonds, salt, herbs and lemon juice in a food processor or blender and process until smooth (about 3 minutes). Add the roasted garlic and pulse until thoroughly combined.

Transfer the dip to a serving bowl. Top with a drizzle of olive oil, the roasted tomatoes and pine nuts, and sprinkle with chilli flakes, if desired. Spread on crusty sourdough, dollop on roasted vegetables or serve with crackers and veggie sticks. Store any leftovers in a sealed container in the fridge for up to 5 days.

MAKES 2 CUPS. GF

KALE CHIPPIES TWO WAYS

Kale is a dark leafy green that contains good amounts of iron and calcium, as well as vitamins A, C and K. It can taste a bit bitter raw, so most people prefer it cooked. If you're still on the fence about kale, I guarantee you'll be hooked once you try these crunchy, delicious chips. I was so happy when I discovered that Alex (a former kale-hater) was cooking these every night while I was away for work, and even happier when I learned that he'd even shown his mum how to make them! Serve these as an appetiser or a side (an easy cheat to increase your green veg intake!). My fave way to enjoy them is with a big bowl of soup.

10 kale leaves, any variety, stems removed, torn
1 tablespoon extra-virgin olive oil
pinch of salt
2 teaspoons nutritional yeast
½ teaspoon smoked paprika

Preheat the oven to 160°C fan-forced (180°C conventional).

Place the kale in a mixing bowl with the oil and salt and toss to coat. Spread over two baking trays. Sprinkle the kale on one tray with nutritional yeast and the other with paprika. Bake for 10 minutes, or until crispy. Keep an eye on them as they can burn pretty quickly. Eat immediately!

SERVES 4 AS A SIDE, GF

CRISPY SWEET POTATO CHIPS

I'm always asked how I get my chips so crispy without a deep-fryer. It's all about how you cut them, coat them and cook them. Orange sweet potatoes are the most difficult to get crispy, as they have a much softer texture when cooked: White and purple varieties have a higher starch content and hold their shape better. Sweet potatoes are not only delicious but are high in beta carotene, which is a precursor for vitamin A. Always keep the skin on, as it contains fibre and other nutrients — just give it a good scrub first.

1 kg sweet potatoes (any variety), scrubbed
1 tablespoon extra-virgin olive oil
1 teaspoon paprika (sweet or smoked)
1 teaspoon salt
1 tablespoon instant polenta or cornmeal

Preheat the oven to 180°C fan-forced (200°C conventional).

Cut the sweet potatoes into long, 2 cm thick batons (keeping them thick ensures they remain firm while cooking). Transfer to a mixing bowl and drizzle over the oil, massaging until each baton is evenly coated. Sprinkle over the paprika, salt and polenta or cornmeal and gently toss to coat.

Place the sweet potato batons on a lined baking tray, ensuring there is a gap between each one. Bake for 25 minutes, or until golden on the outside and fluffy inside. Serve as a side for a leafy salad, or as dippers with soup or any of the dips in this section — dipping them in the Creamy Guacamole (see recipe page 298) is especially yummy!

SERVES 4 AS A SIDE, GF

CHICKPEA FLATBREAD

Chickpea flour (also known as besan flour) is naturally gluten free, and its high protein content will keep you feeling fuller for longer. My favourite way to eat this bread is torn up and dunked in curries and soups. Try experimenting with different herbs and spices to change the flavour. I add fennel seeds to mine, as it reminds me of the freshly made bread rolls served in a lovely vegetarian restaurant I visited in Italy.

1 cup (150 g) chickpea flour
1 teaspoon extra-virgin olive oil
1 teaspoon fennel seeds
½ teaspoon garlic flakes
pinch of salt

Preheat the oven to 180°C fan-forced (200°C conventional) and line a baking tray with baking paper.

In a bowl, whisk together the flour and ¾ cup of water and set aside for 10 minutes.

When the batter has thickened, pour it onto the prepared tray. Drizzle over the oil and sprinkle with the fennel seeds, garlic flakes and salt. Bake for 20–25 minutes, or until golden and crisp around the edges. Serve warm, sliced or torn, with dips or soup.

SERVES 4 AS A SIDE. GF

GREEN TROFIE

I was inspired to give this a go after eating handmade green pasta on my recent travels to Italy. Trofie is a short, twisted pasta from Liguria in northern Italy. You don't need any fancy equipment, not even a rolling pin! It's fiddly but fun – get the whole family or your housemates to help. The iron-rich spinach gives it its gorgeous green colour, plus I've used wholemeal flour to bump up the fibre content. This pasta is delicious with pesto (see recipe page 303) or tossed through my Gorgeous Green Pesto Salad (see recipe page 120).

heaped ¾ cup (130 g) wholemeal spelt flour, sifted,
    plus extra if needed
80 g baby spinach leaves
pinch of salt

Place all the ingredients in a food processor and process until the mixture clumps together to form a smooth, green dough.

Turn the dough out onto a clean, floured surface. If the dough feels sticky, sprinkle over 1–2 teaspoons of flour and knead briefly to combine.

Roll the dough into a long log and cut it into eight even-sized pieces, and cut each piece into four. (You'll now have 32 pieces.)

Now roll each of the 32 pieces into long, thin worms (approximately 2–3 mm thick). Then cut each into segments 3–4 cm long.

Take one segment and roll the ends into points. Press two fingers in the centre to flatten slightly. Now hold the ends, twist the pasta and set aside on a tray, ensuring the pieces don't touch.

Continue rolling, flattening and twirling the remaining segments until you have used up all the pasta dough.

Bring a large saucepan of salted water to the boil over a high heat. Add the fresh pasta, return to the boil and cook for 3–4 minutes. Remove a piece of pasta from the pot and test that it's al dente. Drain and serve with pesto and a green salad.

SERVES 3–4

NUT AND SEED CRACKERS

Nuts and seeds are important components of a healthy diet. They contain healthy fats, which can reduce your risk of heart disease, as well as protein and fibre, which keep you feeling much more satisfied after a meal. These crackers are a delicious snack you can prepare for lunches during the week or use for a weekend platter with dips. My favourite way to have these is topped with avocado, tomato and Beetroot Sauerkraut (see recipe page 332).

½ cup almonds, pre-soaked (see page 18)
½ cup walnuts, pre-soaked (see page 18)
½ cup sunflower seeds, pre-soaked (see page 18)
½ cup flaxseeds
½ cup sesame seeds
1 tablespoon dried Italian herbs
1 cup dehydrated tomatoes (see Tip)

TIP
Dehydrated tomatoes can be found in bulk wholefood stores in the dried fruit section. If you can't find any, use the same quantity of sundried tomatoes, drain the oil and omit the 2 tablespoons of water.

Preheat the oven to 120°C fan-forced (140°C conventional) and line a large baking tray with baking paper.

Place all the ingredients in a food processor and blitz until the mixture resembles breadcrumbs. Transfer to a bowl. Add 2 tablespoons of water and combine with your hands until the mixture holds together (add a drop more water if it doesn't).

Place the mixture on the prepared tray and use your hands to press it out to a thickness of about 5 mm. Cut into 5 cm squares. Bake for 15 minutes, or until browned and crispy around the edges.

Remove the crackers from the oven and allow to cool on the tray for 30 minutes. Store in an airtight container in the fridge for up to 1 week.

MAKES 6, GF

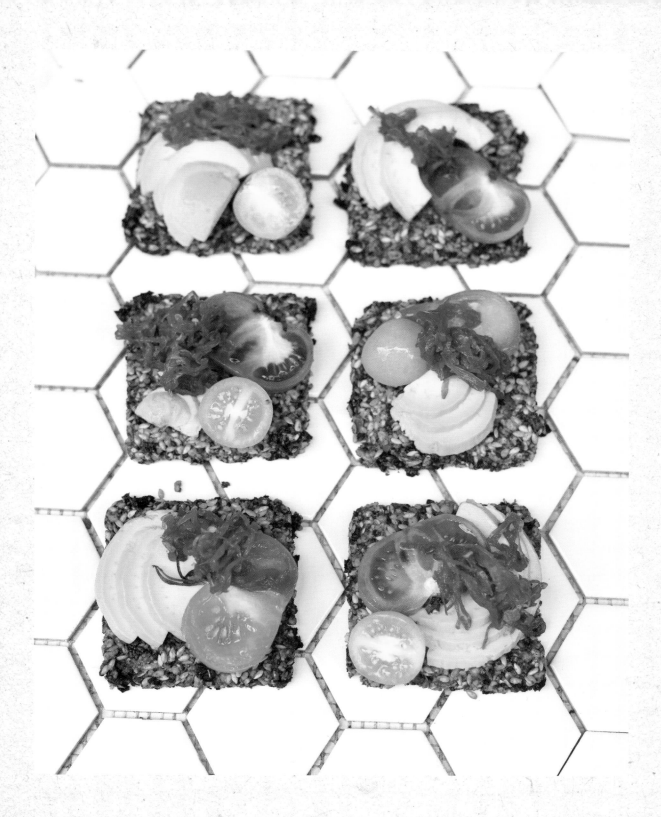

CRISPY CURRIED CHICKPEAS

Roasted curried chickpeas are a really simple and healthy snack idea. Chickpeas are not only an amazing source of vegetable protein but also of fibre and iron. For this reason, legumes such as chickpeas are an essential part of a plant-based diet. These can be eaten as a crunchy snack or tossed through a salad.

1 x 400 g can chickpeas, drained, rinsed and dried
1 teaspoon extra-virgin olive oil
1 teaspoon curry power
pinch of salt

Preheat the oven to 180°C fan-forced (200°C conventional).

Place the chickpeas and oil in a bowl and stir until the chickpeas are well coated. Sprinkle over the curry powder and salt and toss to coat. Transfer to a baking tray and bake for 25 minutes, or until crispy.

These are delicious eaten straight out of the oven, though you can store them in a sealed container in the fridge for up to 4 days.

SERVES 4 AS A SNACK, GF

GREEN CURRY PASTE

Green curry is a spicy Thai curry, the hottest of the three basic types (green, red and yellow). It typically contains fish sauce and shrimp paste (along with palm sugar that's likely to be from non-sustainable sources), so it's pretty difficult to find a store-bought vegan version. That's why I like to make my own and keep it in the fridge, ready to use for curries, stir-fries or noodle soups. There is no sugar added, so if you like a little sweetness in your curry, you can stir in some coconut sugar to taste.

2 long green chillies, roughly chopped
pinch of chilli flakes
3 garlic cloves, peeled
2 spring onions, roughly chopped
¼ cup chopped coriander leaves and stems
4 kaffir lime leaves
1 lemongrass stalk, white part only, roughly chopped
1 teaspoon ground coriander
1 teaspoon cumin seeds
½ teaspoon black peppercorns
1 teaspoon ground galangal
2 tablespoons sesame oil, plus extra
¼ cup tamari
zest of 1 lime

Place all the ingredients in a blender or food processor with ⅓ cup of water. Blend for 2–3 minutes, or until smooth. Transfer to a clean jar and cover the surface with extra sesame oil and a layer of plastic wrap. This will keep for a couple of weeks in the fridge.

MAKES 200 G, GF

TIP
Galangal is from the same family as ginger, though has a more subtle, earthy flavour. It's widely used in Thai and South-East Asian cooking and is available in ground form in most Asian supermarkets. If you can't find any, use ¾ teaspoon of ground ginger instead.

NO-SUGAR TOMATO RELISH

This delicious tomato relish is simple to make, naturally sweet and a much healthier alternative to store-bought versions, some of which contain more than 50 per cent added sugar! Since this recipe uses no sugar or other preservatives, you'll need to keep it in the fridge and use it within 5 days. Serve it with veggie patties, spread on toast or as a dip.

250 g cherry tomatoes, halved
1 tablespoon sultanas
1 teaspoon mustard seeds
1 teaspoon chia seeds

TIP

If you like a spicier relish, simply add some fresh chilli to the pan when you're cooking the tomatoes — a long red cayenne chilli should do the trick, though if you're a hothead you might prefer a bird's eye or habañero.

Place the cherry tomatoes, sultanas and mustard seeds in a saucepan with ½ cup of water. Bring to the boil, reduce the heat and simmer, uncovered, for 15 minutes, or until the liquid has thickened. Transfer to a blender with the chia seeds and process until the relish reaches the desired consistency. (You'll only need to pulse it a few times if you like it chunky.) Transfer to a clean jar, seal and store in the fridge for up to 5 days.

MAKES 300 G. GF

BEETROOT SAUERKRAUT

Sauerkraut is cabbage fermented in brine — a centuries old process for preserving veggies that also happens to be super healthy. The good bacteria that naturally live on veggies thrive in salty water, eating up the sugars to create loads of probiotics. There are many different flavours you can create with sauerkraut, but this one is my absolute fave. The beetroot adds a gentle sweetness, and the ginger gives it a little spicy hit, both of which work well to balance the sourness of the fermented cabbage. You'll need a 2 litre jar (or two 1 litre jars) for this recipe.

½ head red cabbage (about 450 g), finely shredded
1 beetroot (about 180 g), grated
7 cm piece of ginger, peeled and grated
3 teaspoons sea salt
3 cups tepid water

Place the cabbage, beetroot and ginger in a large mixing bowl. Using the back of a large spoon, a pestle or your hands, press or squeeze the vegetables for 3–4 minutes until they soften and begin to give up their juices. Transfer to a sterilised 2 litre jar (or two 1 litre jars).

Place the salt and water in a jug and stir until dissolved. Pour into the jar (or jars), pressing the vegetables down so that they are fully submerged. (If they are not completely covered, add extra brine made from 1 cup of tepid water mixed with 1 teaspoon of salt.) Leave about 3 cm of space at the top of the jar.

Seal loosely with a lid and leave in a shaded area at room temperature for approximately 7 days, or until the mixture has bubbled and tastes sour. Check on it daily to ensure the veggies stay submerged. Once fermented, place in the fridge for up to 2 months.

Serve your sauerkraut on toast with avocado (it tastes great with my herby pumpkin loaf, see recipe page 42), on salads or as a condiment with curries.

MAKES ABOUT 1.5 KG. GF

TIP
If white mould appears on the top it will probably be because the veggies peeped out of the brine. If this happens, simply scoop the mouldy bits out with a spoon and discard. Try placing a smaller jar or a shot glass on top of the veggies to hold them down.

THANK YOU

Creating this book has been my most challenging and exciting project yet. It is a dream come true! I am so grateful to be able to share my wholesome life with you all through my pictures, recipes and words. I would like to personally thank all the people who have been involved in making this book; without you it would not have been possible.

Mary Small, you have turned my dream into a reality; finding my blog and seeing the potential in me to become a published author has changed my life. I couldn't be more thankful for your belief in me.

Clare Marshall, it is such a pleasure to work with you; your patience with me, kindness with words and constant support. You have brought this dream to life and helped me create a piece of work that is truly me.

Miriam Cannell, my wonderful editor, you have really helped my words come to life! And made my writing sound so much more professional. Thank you for all of your help.

Arielle Gamble, the talented designer and illustrator, you have added so much colour and fun to the book. The texts and illustrations you designed have really embodied the wholesome, vibrant and fun life that I wanted to share.

A big thank you to everyone involved in our cover shoot day! Clare Marshall, your planning and organisation made it all come together so perfectly. My hair and make-up gal Luciana Rose, you made me feel bronzed and beautiful all day. Photographer Armelle Habib, your energy and confidence behind the lens kept me going and made me feel like a star. Jason Moss from Byron Kombi Limo, thank you for supplying the dreamiest Kombi, assisting on the day and lending out your home for my hair and make-up session.

And Nicky McLaughlin and the team from Byron Bay Crew, you were so helpful all day long, keeping me hydrated and shaded. It was a big day, and we battled the wind and sun to create a cover that I am so over the moon with!

Alex, my partner in life and soul mate. Thank you for your patience with me while I dedicated every spare hour to creating this book, rather than lazing down at the beach with you. Your assistance in helping me set up my photoshoots, cleaning up my piles of dirty dishes, eating every failed and successful recipe attempt and, most importantly, encouraging and supporting me with all of your love and hugs, always.

Lauren, my other half (literally). Even though you were worlds away through the creation of this book, you were there for me over the phone every single day, encouraging me and inspiring me to chase my dream.

Mum and Dad, thank you both for always believing in me, for giving me the confidence to say yes to every opportunity and for loving me. I love you both!

Family and friends, there are so many of you that I can't thank you all individually, but you have all inspired my recipes through the memories we have created together, the meals we have shared and the knowledge you have shared with me. Thank you for the random texts of encouragement or the tasting of my recipes.

My followers and fellow Insta-foodies, you are my biggest source of inspiration and the reason I am able to create this book. Thank you for all the likes and comments and the constant support. To be able to create and work doing something I love is an absolute dream, and it has all become possible because of each of you … Thank you!

INDEX

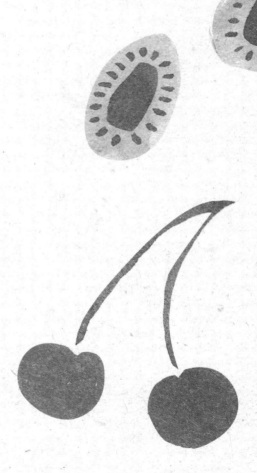

A PLUM BOOK

First published in 2017 by
Pan Macmillan Australia Pty Limited
Level 25, 1 Market Street,
Sydney, NSW 2000, Australia

Level 3, 112 Wellington Parade,
East Melbourne, VIC 3002, Australia

Design and illustrations by Arielle Gamble
Edited by Miriam Cannell
Index by Frances Paterson
Photography by Ellie Bullen (with additional photography by Armelle Habib)
Prop and food styling by Ellie Bullen
Food preparation by Ellie Bullen
Typeset by Arielle Gamble
Colour reproduction by Splitting Image Colour Studio
Printed and bound in China by Imago Printing International Limited

A CIP catalogue record for this book is available from the National Library of Australia.

The publisher would like to thank the following for their generosity in providing props and clothing
for the book: Bridget Bodenham, Mister Zimi and Spell Byron Bay.

5 7 9 10 8 6